LUTHER
AND CALVIN:
RELIGIOUS
REVOLUTIONARIES

For
Bruce McCormack,
inspirational teacher, scholar, friend

LUTHER AND CALVIN: RELIGIOUS REVOLUTIONARIES

Charlotte Methuen

LION

A Lion Book
an imprint of
Lion Hudson plc
Wilkinson House, Jordan Hill Road,
Oxford OX2 8DR, England
www.lionhudson.com
ISBN 978 0 7459 5340 3 (print)
ISBN 978 0 7459 5861 3 (epub)
ISBN 978 0 7459 5860 6 (Kindle)
ISBN 978 0 7459 5862 0 (pdf)

Distributed by:
UK: Marston Book Services, PO Box 269, Abingdon, Oxon, OX14 4YN
USA: Trafalgar Square Publishing, 814 N. Franklin Street, Chicago, IL 60610
USA Christian Market: Kregel Publications, PO Box 2607, Grand Rapids, Michigan 49501

First edition 2011
10 9 8 7 6 5 4 3 2 1 0
First electronic edition 2011

Acknowledgments
Scripture quotations are from The New Revised Standard Version of the Bible copyright ©
1989 by the Division of Christian Education of the National Council of Churches in the
USA. Used by permission. All Rights Reserved.

Note: Many Bible passages are not drawn from any particular translation, since they are
translations of the translations that Luther and Calvin were using: sometimes in German or
French, sometimes from the Vulgate, sometimes from Erasmus.

A catalogue record for this book is available
from the British Library

Typeset in 12/15 Adobe Garamond Pro
Printed and bound in Great Britain by MPG Books

For a full list of references for the quoted material in this work please visit
Charlotte's webpage: www.charlotte-methuen.de and follow the link to
"Luther and Calvin – footnotes".

CONTENTS

INTRODUCTION

The sixteenth century was a time of massive change in Western Europe, and much of that change focused on the church. Although there had been regional variations in the medieval church, its structures and in theory its beliefs were shared by all Western Christians. In 1500 there was really no religious choice. By 1600 that had changed. Different places had different churches, which had different structures, whose buildings looked very different, and whose theology, ideas and practices varied hugely. People still might not have had much choice about whether to be Catholic or Protestant – and if so, what sort of Protestant – but most would have known that other kinds of Christians existed. The structures and ways of doing things which were normal for people in 1500 had been questioned and, in some places, swept away. At the centre of these changes were two reformers: Martin Luther and John Calvin. Between them, they brought about and then helped to stabilize the Reformation – which in modern parlance we might term a revolution – in the way that religion shaped people's lives.

This book offers an introduction to the lives and ideas of Luther and Calvin. It sets each in his historical context and explores some of the ways that their theology was shaped, encouraged, but also constrained by the circumstances in which they lived. One aspect of this is seeing how their theology changed in the course of their careers. This is particularly true of Martin Luther. Luther was a whole generation older than John Calvin, and his theology grew and developed as he began to understand and struggle with the consequence of the stance he took against the Roman church. In this, Luther was like the other reformers of the 1520s who lived through the extraordinary experience of realizing that there could be a church other than that which had shaped the religious existence of Western Europe. They had to work out what it meant to talk about the church in these circumstances, and how to think about authority and truth without reference to a clerical hierarchy. Luther, a lecturer at the University of Wittenberg in Saxony, became an acknowledged leader in this movement. The decisions he made about theology and practice would influence many Christians in his generation. However, not everyone agreed with him, and by the end of the 1520s, it was clear that divisions were emerging within the Reformation movement, particularly between Luther and Huldrych Zwingli, the leader of the Reformation in Zürich. Honed in the 1530s and 1540s, Luther's theology would prove deeply influential not only in his native Saxony, but in many German-speaking lands and in Scandinavia, whence it would be exported in various forms to colonies around the world.

By the time Calvin began to explore theological ideas in the late 1520s and early 1530s, the Reformation had taken hold and was clearly a force to be reckoned with. Once he was converted to Reformation ideas, Calvin had the works of the first generation to read, and read them he clearly did. His theological system emerged in a mature form which would have been unthinkable in the previous generation. Calvin's attempts to mediate between the different parties of the Reformation – particularly between Zürich and Wittenberg – would be ultimately unsuccessful, but they shaped his theology. So too did his particular experiences of the church: of persecution in France and of exile in Strasbourg and Geneva. Calvin's theology would be influential in Switzerland, in France, in

England, in Scotland, in the newly formed Netherlands, and in parts of Hungary and some of the German lands. It would also prove inspirational for a generation of Christians who would draw on it to oppose the state-defined religion of their native countries. Calvinist radicals, often known as Puritans to the English-speaking world, took their theology with them into exile in North America, or in southern Africa. In particular, Calvin's theology was highly influential in many of the first colonies in North America, and helped shape the religious culture of the United States of America. In the eighteenth and nineteenth centuries, colonial and missionary interests coupled with emigration took the ideas of Luther and Calvin into Asia, Africa, North America and Australia. Luther's and Calvin's ideas thus fertilized the roots of the Protestant thought and culture which shaped so many aspects of political and intellectual life across the modern world.

My intention in this book has been to allow Luther and Calvin to speak as much as possible in their own words. Since Luther wrote in German and Latin, and Calvin in French and Latin, English translations have necessarily had to be used. Many of Luther's works have been published in English translation in *Luther's Works* (St Louis: Concordia, 1974). Most of the exploration of Calvin's theology is drawn from three different editions of his *Institutes of Christian Religion*: the first Latin edition of 1536, the first French edition of 1541, and the final Latin edition to appear in his lifetime, of 1559. These translations do not all observe the same conventions, whether referring to God (as He or as he), or in referring to human beings (as people or as men). Quotations follow the conventions of the translation, and are therefore inconsistent between translations.

This book would not have been possible without the engaged interest of several generations of my students, in seminars at the University of the Ruhr in Bochum, in the Luther and Calvin classes at the University of Oxford, in the Reformation reading classes at Ripon College Cuddesdon, and those who have grappled with Luther's and Calvin's theology in studying the Reformation. I have benefited enormously from their careful reading of source texts and their probing questions of interpretation. Thanks are due also to my colleagues in Bochum, Professor Dr Christoph Strohm and Dr Judith Becker, both of whom helped me understand Luther and Calvin better. Professor Diarmaid MacCulloch, Professor Sarah Foot, and Dr Sarah Apetrei at Oxford have been greatly supportive during the time in Oxford which gave rise to this project. My husband, Robert Franke, has been a keen advocate of the book. Kate Kirkpatrick, Alison Hull, Sheila Jacobs, and Jessica Tinker, my editors at Lion Hudson, have been encouraging, patient and endlessly helpful. I am particularly grateful to those who read and commented on the earlier drafts: Betsy Gray-Hammond, David Hicks, Isabella Image, Michael Leyden, Jane Methuen, Elizabeth Muston, Jo Rose, Konstantin Schober, and Rob Wainwright. All have made suggestions which have improved the text greatly. Inaccuracies of course remain my own responsibility.

That I have become so engaged by the thought of the Reformation is ultimately a result of the inspirational teaching of Professor Bruce McCormack, now of Princeton, under whose direction I first read both Luther and Calvin while a student at New College in Edinburgh. This book is dedicated to him with grateful thanks.

PART I

MARTIN LUTHER

CHAPTER 1

LUTHER'S CONTEXT

The late-medieval church in the German lands

The church in the late fifteenth century elicited mixed reactions. Articulate critics such as the Dutch humanist Desiderius Erasmus painted a shocking picture of corruption and excess, with bishops and abbots living lives of luxury, uneducated clerics holding multiple offices, and friars arguing about the number of knots in their belts. There was some truth in these criticisms, especially the first: cardinals and archbishops, bishops, abbots and abbesses wielded considerable influence, both ecclesiastical and political. Indeed, in the German lands of the Holy Roman Empire, the archbishops of Trier, Mainz, and Cologne would cast three of the seven votes which served to elect the emperor. Noble or up-and-coming families might well see such influential posts as appropriate for younger sons, and feel it worth spending a great deal of money to acquire one.

Albrecht of Brandenburg came from such a family. His father was the Elector of Brandenburg, one of the four secular rulers who had a vote in imperial elections, along with the Elector of Saxony, the king of Bohemia, and the Elector of the Palatinate. Albrecht's father died when he was just nine years old. Together with his elder brother, Joachim, who inherited the duchy of Brandenburg and with it the electoral title, Albrecht received a humanist education. In 1506, the brothers founded the University of Frankfurt-an-der-Oder. Albrecht, the younger brother, was destined for a clerical career. In 1509 he was appointed to a canonry at the cathedral in Mainz. In 1513 he was ordained priest, and in that same year made Archbishop of Magdeburg and Administrator of the Diocese of Halberstadt. A year later, aged twenty-four, Albrecht also became Archbishop of Mainz, Imperial Elector and Primate of the German Empire. The debt he and his family incurred in acquiring this, their second imperial electoral title, and paying the fines which allowed Albrecht to break canon law by holding senior posts in three different dioceses, was considerable. It was in the hope of paying off some of this debt that Albrecht applied for permission to preach the indulgence campaign against which, in 1517, Luther would direct his Ninety-Five Theses.

Albrecht's biography illustrates the problem of generalizing about the state of the Church in the early sixteenth century. Although his ecclesiastical offices were bought for him, Albrecht, as we have seen, was humanist educated. He was critical of corruption within the church, and to some extent a reforming bishop. Albrecht shared an interest in and commitment to the church as the means of salvation which was common to many of his contemporaries. Church building flourished in the fifteenth century, paid for by wealthy families, monastic orders, merchants and all manner of other people as a way of glorifying God. Lay involvement in church life took very varied forms. Societies and confraternities for lay people were a central part of the life of almost every parish. Craft guilds financed altars at which masses could be said for their members, whether living or dead. Wealthy families extended churches or built chapels. Princes such as Frederick the Wise, Elector of Saxony, Luther's patron, invested huge amounts in collecting and displaying relics. Local people gave to their parish churches statues of their favoured saints, or clothes and jewellery to decorate them. Societies of men or women, or teenage girls or boys raised money to keep lights burning in front of the statues. Nearly everyone went on pilgrimages according to their means: the wealthy to the Holy Land or to Rome; the less well off to local shrines. In Wittenberg, a great attraction was the amazing collection of relics assembled by Frederick the Wise. A properly prayerful tour of this collection could secure the pilgrim a reduction of hundreds of years off their time in purgatory.

Late-medieval people were avid to assure themselves of their salvation, and the church offered ways for them to gain that assurance, generally to the great financial benefit of the church and the clergy. The piety of many people centred on the mass, and in particular the visual moment at which the priest elevated the unleavened communion bread – the host, which had now become the body of Christ – for all to see. Most people went only to look, and actually received communion – offered to them in the form of the bread – only annually, if at all. The celebration of mass, however, was frequent. Indeed, in larger churches or cathedrals with many chapels and altars, several masses would often be being said at different altars at the same time, offered for the benefit of souls in purgatory, and paid for by funds given to the church by relatives or left by the beneficiary themselves. The Latin words were not always understood particularly well by the priest himself, who might have received a minimal education. They were spoken under his breath at an altar obscured by a screen, on top of which a cross was placed – the rood screen. A bell, rung at the most holy points of the mass – the consecration and the moment of elevation – alerted the people in the church that these points had been reached. Sometimes there might be no congregation present. In churches with multiple altars, the congregation might move from altar to altar as they heard the ringing of the bells, hoping to catch a glimpse of the body of Christ in the hands of the priest. The literate and pious might pray before an image, or study a popular devotional work such as Thomas à Kempis's *Imitation of Christ*, looking up when the bell rang and being assured of Christ's presence with them. The illiterate could puzzle out the biblical stories painted on the walls of the church.

Piety and devotion were an important aspect of many people's lives, as shown by the popularity of religious works and of personal religious images. Those who wished to understand more about their faith might study and pray together. Some formed religious communities and lived together without taking life vows; one of the more widespread groups was the Brothers of the Common Life. The growth in popular piety was not unrelated to humanism. It came to be known as the modern devotion, or *devotio moderna*.

The saying of frequent masses was supported by endowment from the faithful which not only paid the livings of many priests, but was put to use in supporting education and church embellishment or refurbishment. In a society in which money was by no means the only medium of trade, endowing masses often meant the transfer of goods or land to the church. Gifts of land not only benefited the institutions of the church, but removed that land from the jurisdictions of local princes, who under the terms of canon law were unable to tax income arising from church lands. The fulfilment of the church's promise of repose for the souls of its people came at a cost of property in this world to families and local rulers, and some of them were beginning to resent it. Princes had good economic reasons for seeking to wrest back land from the church, or at the least negotiating rights to some proportion of the taxes levied by Rome on income from ecclesiastical property, which were known as annates. In Spain in the late fifteenth century, and in France in the early sixteenth, monarchs signed agreements with the papacy which allowed them to do that, and which also allowed them to determine the candidates for senior church appointments. In the German lands there was resentment that Italian noblemen were too often given prime ecclesiastical posts, but the political system there made the situation difficult to change. The emperor's authority was more indirect than that of the monarchs in Spain or in France. The rulers of local German territories were subject in different ways to both emperor and pope; increasingly they sought to assert their independence of both. This would be a crucial factor in protecting Luther from both papal and imperial punishment.

Criticism of the church was nothing new, but the growth of towns through the late Middle Ages had brought with it a growing need for people who could read and write to serve civic functions, and to work in crafts and trades. The new city and town councils saw education as part of their responsibility to their communities, and the establishment of new schools to some extent removed responsibility for education from religious orders. Education still tended to have a definite Christian aspect, but the Renaissance interest in the texts of classical Greek and Roman culture was a strong influence on humanist learning. Boys – and, to a far lesser extent, girls – were taught Latin according to the rhetoric and style of Cicero rather than the barbaric Latin (as it was coming to be seen) of the Middle Ages. Members of this new educated class had access to a growing range of texts which were emerging from the newly invented printing presses. These were the people who were most likely to give money and endowments to the church, but they were also able, and increasingly willing, to think critically about the institution to which they were giving, and to make new demands of it. They expected the church to educate them in matters of salvation, and if those employed by the church could not or would not, then they would take steps themselves.

By the end of the fifteenth century, a number of town and city councils across the German lands, and particularly those of the imperial free cities, which were largely self-governing, were employing a friar or a secular priest to preach to the people in the vernacular. It might even be laid down that the city preacher's words should be *evangelisch* – evangelical, literally, "of the Gospel" – in response to the growing influence of biblical humanists. City councils sought to demonstrate their ability to exercise responsibility for the well-being of their people, often asserting their independence against a bishop who sought to retain his authority over them in matters both spiritual and temporal. Consequently, the Reformation frequently took hold in towns and cities. Huldrych Zwingli's

Zürich, Martin Bucer's Strasbourg, and later John Calvin's Geneva were notable examples among many others.

The late medieval church was an integral part of a society in which people saw considerable continuity between this world and the next. People knew that what they did could affect their salvation, and the teaching and practices of the church encouraged this belief and codified it, offering ways of reckoning up grace against sin. It was this world into which Martin Luther was born, this world which he would encounter in his time as a monk, and this world against which he would rebel, splitting the Western church.

Martin Luther: From childhood to professor of theology

Martin Luther was born on 10 November 1483 in Eisleben in Thuringia to Hans Ludher (as he spelt his surname), the second son of a family which owned a farm in Möhra, near Eisenach, and his wife Margarethe Lindemann, whose family also came from Eisenach. He was baptized the next day, on 11 November, St Martin's Day, and given the name of the saint. Soon afterwards, the family moved to Mansfeld, where Hans Ludher managed a series of copper mines. Luther attended the *Trivialschule* or elementary school in Mansfeld from the age of about seven, where he would have learnt the classical *trivium*: grammar, rhetoric and logic, all taught in Latin. When he was about fourteen, he was sent to the cathedral school in Magdeburg, where he boarded with the Brothers of the Common Life. A year later, in 1498, he moved on to St George's parish school in Eisenach, where he seems to have been impressed by the spiritual depth of Johannes Braun, one of the priests. In the spring of 1501, Luther signed the matriculation book for the Arts Faculty at the University of Erfurt: *Martinus ludher ex mansfelt*. Here he was introduced to the so-called "modern way", the *via moderna* or nominalist school, of philosophy. He studied the works of Aristotle, and particularly the Nichomachean Ethics. In 1502 he was awarded his *Baccalaureus Artium* or Bachelor of Arts, and in January 1505 his *Magister Artium*, or Master of Arts, placed second in his class. Luther was later to be extremely critical of the medieval system of education, believing that it led people away from a dependence on the Gospel and grace to a belief that they could play a part in their own salvation. But there can be no doubt that Luther's own education equipped him well. He acquired good Latin, a love of Latin poetry, and an appreciation of the importance of definitions and of logical arguments, all of which would be most useful to him in his career as a reformer.

For the 21-year-old Luther, however, no such ambitions were in the air. Following his father's plans for him, in May 1505 he began to study law. He seems to have had doubts about this choice from the start. An outbreak of plague or another epidemic illness confronted him with death, and made him fearful for the state of his soul. Returning from a visit to Mansfeld on 2 June 1505, he narrowly escaped being struck by lightning, praying to St Anne, the mother of the Virgin Mary: "Help me, and I will become a monk." Despite the disapproval of his father, just six weeks later, on 17 July, Luther applied to the Erfurt house of the observant Augustinian hermits, entering the order later that autumn.

As a novice, Luther dedicated himself to keeping the rule. Prayer, fasting, regular self-examination and confession to a superior were an integral part of his life. Despite his efforts, however – and both Luther and his superiors remembered him as extremely, even overly, conscientious in all that he did as a monk – Luther was unable to experience a sense of certainty that he was saved. His situation was made more complicated by the decision of his superiors in 1506 that he should prepare for ordination to the priesthood. As part of his preparation he read the *Explication of the Canon of the Mass* by Gabriel Biel, which emphasized the importance of a precisely correct manner of celebration and the need for the priest to be at one with God. This increased Luther's sense of inadequacy and unworthiness, and his first mass on 2 May 1507 was a difficult experience. Over the years that followed, his fears and uncertainties – what he called his *Anfechtungen* – shook his confidence in all that he had been taught about how salvation might be achieved.

During his novitiate, Luther also began to study the Scriptures. It is possible that he encountered a Bible for the first time in 1505, perhaps on entering the monastery, although it may simply be that this was the first time he had had an opportunity to read biblical texts without the textual glosses and commentaries commonly found in medieval Bibles. His interest and ability were such that after his ordination Luther was instructed by Johann von Staupitz, Vicar General of the Augustinians in Germany, and the "Professor for Bible" at the University of Wittenberg, to take up the study of theology at the University of Erfurt. At the same time, he was made responsible for teaching philosophy to students in the Augustinian house. He was clearly successful, for in 1508 he was sent to the University of Wittenberg to share responsibility for teaching philosophy there, while continuing with his own studies. In 1509 he was awarded his *Baccalaureus biblicus*, or bachelor of the Bible, in Wittenberg, and later that year his

Baccalaureus sententiarius, or bachelor of the Sentences, in Erfurt. The first of these degrees qualified Luther to lecture on the Bible; the second to lecture on Peter Lombard's *Sentences*, the standard medieval textbook which for most medieval students of theology was the key to understanding theological – and, with it, biblical – truth.

Before he took up a teaching post, however, Luther went to Rome. Staupitz was seeking to reunite the different strands of the Augustinian order in Germany, and the Augustinian house in Erfurt had opposed his efforts. In 1510 Luther was sent as a representative of those opposing voices to negotiate with the head of the order in Rome. He seems to have been struck both by the amazing range of possibilities – holy places, pilgrimages, relics, masses, and simply the churches – offered by Rome to the pilgrim, of which he made full use, and also by the extravagant and corrupt pomp which surrounded the papal court. In the short term, Luther came to be convinced that Staupitz's endeavours should be supported rather than opposed. On their return to Germany, Staupitz, whose other commitments had never given him time to take seriously his responsibilities as Professor for Bible at Wittenberg, sent Luther to take over that post.

This appointment, which Luther took up in 1512, marked the beginning of a long association between Luther, the University of Wittenberg and the successive Electors of Saxony: at this time Frederick "the Wise"; from 1525, his brother John "the Steadfast" or "the Constant"; and finally, from 1532, John's son John Frederick "the Magnanimous". The University of Wittenberg had been founded in 1502 by Elector Frederick. At the same time, an Augustinian monastery had been established, in which Luther now lived. Luther was awarded his Doctorate in Theology in October 1512, taking an oath in which – among other things – he swore that he would preach and teach the Scriptures faithfully. Luther would hold the post of Professor for Bible for the rest of his life.

He began, in 1513, by lecturing on the Psalms. In 1515 he started to lecture on Romans, turning to Galatians in 1516, and to Hebrews in 1517. Luther's lectures, especially those on the Psalms and Romans, witness to the development in his thought on matters of free will and justification, and his moving away from scholastic methods of interpreting Scripture. From 1514 he was also preaching regularly in the town church, appointed by the council, where he preached generally on the Gospel set for the day in the morning and on the Epistle in the afternoon. Through his lectures and sermons, Luther was engaging with the text in both German and Latin, both for students and for the people of Wittenberg, and was beginning to develop a personal, meditative approach to the reading of Scripture. In this he was influenced by his discovery of German mysticism. In 1516 Luther published an initial, incomplete edition of the *Theologia Deutsch*, or *German Theology*, which he erroneously believed to have been written by the German mystic Johannes Tauler. The importance of this work to him is illustrated by his introduction to the complete edition, published in 1518, "I thank God that I have found and heard my God in the German tongue, as neither I nor they [that is, scholastic theologians] have yet found him in the Latin, Greek, or Hebrew tongue."

By 1516, Luther was beginning to explore in his preaching his concerns at the misunderstanding and abuse of indulgences, and to engage in his university teaching with questions about free will, grace, and salvation. This is apparent from the text of a disputation on these themes over which he presided in late

1516. He was also preparing a collection of German sermons on the penitential psalms (Psalms 6, 32, 38, 51, 102, 130, and 143), "not for well educated Nurembergers, but for raw Saxons". This, the first of his own writings to be published, was printed in Wittenberg in the spring of 1517, and reprinted at Leipzig within the year. Soon afterwards, Luther wrote to John Lang, the prior of his former house in Erfurt:

> Our theology and that of St Augustine, by the grace of God, are making rapid progress in our university. Aristotle continues to fall from his throne, and his end is only a matter of time. All object to hearing lectures on the Sentences, and those who want an audience must expound this theology – that is, of the Bible, or of St Augustine, or one of the other respected church authorities.

That summer, Luther was disputing in the university against scholastic theology. He was becoming known in Wittenberg for his criticisms of scholastic theology, and many of his colleagues were beginning to agree.

The indulgence crisis and its repercussions

Indulgences are a way of replacing a personal or direct form of penance with an action, offered to the church for some worthy cause, and often, but not always, taking the form of a financial contribution. The first Jubilee indulgence was issued by Pope Boniface VIII in 1300, and proved such a profitable source of income for the papacy that Jubilee indulgences soon became quite a regular occurrence. The underlying theology, based on a treatise by Alexander Hales, was explicated in the Bull

Unigenitus, proclaimed by Pope Clement VI in 1343, which argued that Christ, through his death, had given to the church a great treasure of merit, which was increased by the good deeds of Mary, the saints and all the elect, and which could be dispensed by Peter and by Peter's successors – the popes – to the faithful. By the mid-fifteenth century, indulgences could be acquired not only for the soul of the giver, but also for the souls of his or her relatives or friends. Pope Sixtus IV made the intention quite explicit in his Bull *Salvator Noster*, proclaimed in August 1476:

> If any parents, friends, or other Christians are moved by obligation of piety towards those very souls who are exposed to the fire of purgatory for the expiation of punishments which by divine justice are their due, let them during the stated period of ten years give a fixed amount or value of money, as laid down by its dean and chapter or by our own collector, for the repair of the Church of Saints, paying either in person at the Church or by duly accredited messengers, it is then our will that plenary remission should avail by intercession for the said souls in purgatory, to win them relief from their punishments – the souls, that is, for whose sakes the stated value or quantity of money have been paid in the manner declared.

With *Salvator Noster*, the preaching of indulgences clearly became a way of raising funds for the church. Indulgences were issued by the pope for a specific cause. Permission was then given to local bishops, dioceses or even cities to preach the campaign locally, keeping part of the profits for themselves and passing the rest to Rome. When in the late fifteenth century

Strasbourg's city council wished to take greater responsibility for the care of the sick in the city, the councillors applied for, and were granted, permission to preach an indulgence. It was nothing new when in 1507 Pope Julius II issued a Jubilee indulgence for the rebuilding of St Peter's basilica, but it was this indulgence, renewed by Pope Leo X in 1513 and 1515, which would provoke the Reformation.

Leo X's renewal of the Jubilee indulgence brought with it an opportunity for the young Albrecht of Brandenburg, Archbishop of Mainz, to recoup some of the debts he had incurred in acquiring that office. Albrecht was allowed to retain a substantial proportion of the funds which were raised by the preaching of the indulgence in the German lands under his jurisdiction. It was, therefore, in his financial interest to ensure that the campaign was successful. He issued careful instructions, detailing what graces might be expected from the preaching of the indulgence, instructing penitents to visit the churches where the papal arms were set up in order to receive full indulgence for all their sins, and explaining how they could make financial contributions in place of doing their penance in one of those churches, or as part of their negotiations about choice of confessor. To lead the campaign, he appointed the Dominican Johannes Tetzel, an experienced preacher of indulgences. Tetzel's emotive preaching left no doubt about what could be expected: "Do you not hear the voices of your dead parents and other people, who cry out, saying, 'Have mercy, have mercy on me! We are enduring harsh and painful punishment, and you could rescue us with a few alms, but you will not do so.'" This was the approach that Luther would criticize in his Ninety-Five Theses against Indulgences: "They preach only human doctrines who say that as soon as the money clinks into the money chest, the soul flies out of purgatory" (Thesis 27). Tetzel's indulgence campaign arrived in the Archdiocese of Magdeburg in the early autumn of 1517.

Frederick the Wise, however, refused to allow the papal indulgence to be preached in his lands. He had spent much time and money building up an extensive relic collection, which was kept in the castle church at Wittenberg and thrown open to the public twice each year on the second Sunday after Easter and on All Saints' Day. The collection included, among many other relics, "particles" from threads spun by the Virgin Mary, from the house where she lived when she was fourteen years old, from the chamber where she was visited by the angel, from her milk which Jesus suckled as a baby, and from the straw upon which Jesus lay in the manger. Each of these particles – in total 5,005 – was said to remove 100 days from the pilgrim's time in purgatory. By paying to visit the whole collection, and completing all eight "tours", a pilgrim to the collection could amass a total of over 1,373 years off purgatory, together with sixteen weeks of indulgence for someone else. Frederick had little interest in allowing any competition into Saxony. However, their ruler's lack of interest did not stop the burghers of Wittenberg crossing the nearby River Elbe to secure themselves the papal indulgence in one of the churches in Ducal Saxony where Frederick's cousin, Duke George, had allowed it to be preached.

Contemporary woodcuts show indulgence preachers displaying the papal arms prominently before the cross, and setting up tables to count the money offered by the faithful. Such images were intended to remind those who knew their Bible of the money lenders in the Temple. For Luther, such preaching was not only in itself a desecration of the Gospel, but gave those who responded to it an entirely false sense of security. He had come to be convinced that contrition must imply change of life and although, as will be discussed below, it is not clear that he had already come to hold the doctrine of justification by grace through faith alone, he was certainly already convinced that it was a believer's faith and their active love of neighbour, rather than any programmatic tasks or payments set them by the church, which would assure them of salvation. Luther was familiar with an important humanist correction to the Latin translation of Matthew 4:17, which observed that the meaning of the Greek was more correctly translated "Repent" than "Do penance". He had come to believe that the task of the believer was not to undertake acts of penance, but to live a life of repentance. This was the content of the first of the list of ninety-five theses which he drew up for a proposed *Disputation on the Value of Indulgences*. On 31 October 1517 he sent the list, with a covering letter, to Albrecht of Brandenburg, the Archbishop of Mainz. Whether Luther also nailed the theses to the door of Wittenberg's castle church is not clear. It would certainly have been normal practice to publicize disputation theses there, but it would also have been usual to wait for a reply from those invited to participate, in this case a representative of the Archbishop of Mainz.

The disputation was never to take place. Albrecht passed Luther's theses on to the University of Mainz for a response, and he also sent a copy to Rome, probably with the support of the Dominicans, encouraged by Tetzel. By February 1518, voices in Rome were demanding that Luther be silenced by his order. Meanwhile, copies of the theses had been printed in Wittenberg and in Nuremberg and were circulating, and a German translation had been made and printed without Luther's permission. His ideas had already begun to reach a wider public than Latin-reading academic circles.

Recognizing the importance of explaining his ideas in the vernacular, Luther wrote a *Sermon on Indulgences and Grace* in German, in which he presented his critique of the preaching of indulgences. It is not clear exactly when the *Sermon* was written, or whether it was ever preached, but it was published in March 1518, with editions printed in Wittenberg, Leipzig, Nuremberg and Augsburg, and achieved wide circulation. At around the same time – in preparation for Lent – Luther's *Short Explanation of the Ten Commandments* was also printed. In this he sought to show more precisely what it meant to make one's whole life one of repentance, and in particular the different ways that it was possible to break the commandments and to keep them.

Luther's ideas were beginning to spread, and his superiors in the Augustinian Order enabled them to spread even further. Faced with a demand from Rome that Luther be silenced, Staupitz instead invited him to speak to the General Congregation of the German Augustinians, which was meeting in Heidelberg in April 1518. Luther defended twenty-eight theological theses and twelve philosophical theses before an audience which included the future reformers Martin Bucer and Johannes Brenz.

In August 1518, Luther was accused of heresy and was called to account for himself in Rome. At this point Frederick the Wise intervened. As an Imperial Elector, at a time when no one could know how long the elderly Emperor Maximilian would live, Frederick had considerable influence. He chose to use it to assert his own authority against that of both the pope and the emperor, by protecting Luther. Frederick insisted that Luther should not be arrested and taken to Rome, but should be questioned on German territory. In October 1518, therefore, Luther was summoned to the Imperial Diet in Augsburg to be cross-examined by the papal legate, Cardinal Thomas Cajetan. Luther defended the views he had put forward in the Ninety-Five Theses, arguing that to suggest the pope controlled access to the treasure of the church – that is, to merit and grace – was unbiblical. Cajetan condemned Luther as a heretic, and instructed Frederick that he should be given up to Rome. Once more, Frederick refused, demanding instead that Luther should be tried by theologians with a good knowledge of the Bible and the Fathers, and not by canon lawyers. In a situation in which Emperor Maximilian himself was canvassing for the support of the Electors for his grandson Charles, king of the recently united kingdom of Spain, it was clear that an imperial election was imminent. The papacy had no wish to antagonize Frederick, and Luther was allowed to return to Wittenberg.

The papacy moves against Luther

At Augsburg, Staupitz had released Luther from his vows of obedience to the Augustinian Order, leaving him free to defend his views, but depriving him of the protection offered by the order. Without Frederick the Wise, Luther's fate would almost certainly have been assured. Like Jan Hus, the Bohemian reformer who had been burnt at the stake at the Council of Constance a century earlier, he would have found himself executed as a heretic. He must have been acutely aware that this fate could become his at any time, especially after his disputation with Johannes Eck, Professor of Theology at

Ingolstadt and a papal legate, at Leipzig in the summer of 1519. Eck had engaged to dispute on free will with Luther's colleague, Andreas Bodenstein von Karlstadt, and insisted that Luther be invited as well, in order to engage with some of his criticisms of the papacy. While the imperial election was taking place in Augsburg, electing Charles emperor on 28 June, Luther was in Leipzig, defending views on the church's authority which, as Eck lost no time in pointing out, were identical to those for which Jan Hus had been condemned by the Council of Constance. Luther maintained his position, arguing that it was based on Scripture, and that the condemnation of Hus indicated that not only the pope, but also councils could err. With this explicit denial of the authority of the medieval church and its institutions, the debate had moved into a new arena. Luther's criticism of the practice of indulgences, which in the Ninety-Five Theses had been carefully phrased so as to allow pope and curia to collude in the suggestion that they knew nothing about what was going on, had now given way to a clear and explicit questioning of papal authority.

Against the backdrop of the growing conflict with Rome, Luther engaged in writing a range of more devotional works directed at helping people to understand more about their faith. The year 1519 saw the first condemnations and burnings of his works by the universities of Cologne and Louvain. It also brought the publication of short catechetical works in German on the Lord's Prayer, confession, baptism and the Lord's Supper, as well as his Galatians commentary, based on lectures given in 1516. In correcting this last work, Luther had the help of the young humanist scholar Philip Melanchthon, who had recently been appointed by Frederick to a post in Wittenberg. Melanchthon's appointment marked the beginning of a process of curriculum reform at the University of Wittenberg which would be driven both by humanist principles and by Luther's theology.

Luther's catechetical works gained a wide circulation across the German-speaking lands. They were followed in 1520 by a series of works written as the process in Rome was moving towards Luther's condemnation. These included what have come to be known as Luther's three Reformation Treatises. The first, published in German in August, was *To the Christian Nobility of the Germany Nation, on the Improvement of the Christian Estate*, a clarion call to the German rulers to reform the church if the church would not reform itself. The second, written in Latin and printed in October, was the theological treatise *On the Babylonian Captivity of the Church: A Prelude*, an exposition of the sacraments which redefined their number, first to three – Eucharist, baptism, and penance – and then to two – Eucharist and baptism. The third, *On the Freedom of a Christian*, or *On Christian Freedom*, written in Latin and dedicated to Pope Leo X in a somewhat spurious attempt to appease him, rolled off the presses in November, with a German translation following almost immediately. This was Luther's first extended discussion of the doctrine of justification by faith alone. The first and last of these three treatises were to become two of the most popular and influential of Luther's works.

Exsurge Domine – Arise, O Lord – the papal Bull condemning Luther and his teachings, was promulgated in Rome on 15 June 1520. It threatened Luther with excommunication if he did not recant within sixty days. However, although it was proclaimed across Germany by Johannes Eck and Jerome Aleander, and Luther's supporters published it in Saxony to increase his popularity, the Bull did not actually reach Luther in Wittenberg until October that year. Once more, Frederick moved to support Luther. In Cologne he conferred with the young Emperor Charles V and with the papal delegates Eck and Aleander, again refusing to send Luther to be tried in Rome. Frederick agreed that Luther should appear before the next Imperial Diet, the first under the new emperor, which was to meet in Worms in 1521. Scarcely was Frederick back in Wittenberg, when on 10 December Luther publicly burned the Bull, together with his copy of Canon Law, and published a treatise in German and in Latin proclaiming that he had done so. On 3 January 1521, Leo X issued the Bull *Decet Romanum* which formally excommunicated Luther.

The Diet of Worms

The Diet of Worms had been intended to begin at Epiphany (6 January) 1521, the feast marking the visit of the three kings to Jesus, in recognition that the new emperor was three times king – of the united Spain, of Naples, and of the Romans. After some delays, it finally opened on 28 January. The Imperial Diet was the primary organ of imperial rule within the Holy Roman Empire. This particular Diet was intended to set up structures which would give more power to the German princes, and put an end to the power struggles between them and the emperor. Most of the German rulers, both secular and ecclesiastical, therefore attended. So too did anyone else who had an interest to present, and those who had business with those who gathered there. Church interests were well represented, for the emperor had the right to fill any senior diocesan or cathedral post within the empire which fell vacant during his first year of office. Merchants gathered in Worms, hoping to attract the custom of the princes and their retinues. Allowing Luther to speak publicly at Worms, his opponents feared, would offer him the chance of expounding his ideas to a broad and possibly susceptible audience. He was summoned to give account of himself in a closed session towards the end of the Diet.

Luther set out for Worms on 2 April. He was welcomed enthusiastically in all the towns he travelled through on his journey, preaching to massive crowds in Erfurt, Gotha and Eisenach, and arrived in Worms on 16 April to considerable acclaim. He was instructed to appear before the Diet the following afternoon. His representative was Jerome Schurff, Professor of Canon Law at Wittenberg. The next day, Luther was brought before the Diet and questioned by Johann von Eck, a senior priest in Trier and representative of the Archbishop of Trier (and not the same Eck against whom Luther had debated at Leipzig). Von Eck asked Luther whether a pile of some twenty-five works was his, and whether he would stand by what he had written in them. Schurff demanded that the titles be read out, and Luther agreed that he was the author of these works. On the second point, Luther requested time for an answer on the question of faith which, he said, was "the most difficult question in the world". After consultation, von Eck responded that although the emperor was surprised that Luther did not have an answer prepared, he might have a further day to consider.

Luther withdrew and spent much of the night in prayer and consultation. The next day, he had his answer ready. Addressing "My lord, most serene Emperor, most illustrious princes, most gracious lords" he apologized for any breach of court etiquette and again declared himself to be the author of the works he had been shown. As to whether he stood by their contents, he asked that it be noted that his books were not all of the same kind.

In some I have dealt with religious faith and morals so simply and evangelically that my very antagonists are compelled to confess that these books are useful, harmless, and fit to be read by all Christians. Even the Bull, savage and cruel as it is, grants that some of my books are harmless, although it condemns them by a judgment that is simply monstrous. If I were to start revoking them, what should I be doing?

A second group of writings consisted of polemic against "the Papacy and the doctrine of the Papists" who had "laid waste all Christendom, body and soul" and had been particularly destructive to the German nation. "If I revoke these books, all I shall achieve is to add strength to tyranny." A third class had been written against individuals. Luther conceded that he had sometimes been "more acrimonious than befits my religion or my calling" but to revoke what he had said would be to accede in what these people were doing. Von Eck, as imperial orator, replied that Luther was not there to question the teachings of the church. Moreover, he was not answering the point. Would he revoke his writings, or would he not? Luther's answer was unequivocal:

Unless I am convinced by the testimony of Scripture of plain reason (for I believe neither in Pope nor councils alone; since it is agreed that they have often erred and contradicted themselves), I am bound by the Scriptures I have quoted, and my conscience is captive to the Word of God. I neither can nor will retract anything, for it is neither safe nor honest to go against one's conscience. Amen.

It is almost certain that Luther did not actually say: "Here I stand – I cannot do otherwise." However, that was certainly the implication of what he is recorded as saying. As he left the room, he was heard to say, "I am finished." Like Hus to the Council of Constance, Luther had come to the Diet of Worms under a month's guarantee of safe passage. Unlike Hus, Luther's safe passage was honoured. He left Worms a week later, on 26 April.

Luther was placed under Imperial Ban on 8 May. Towards the end of that month, as the Diet drew to a close, Charles V issued the Edict of Worms, which condemned Luther and called for him to be executed, condemned also any who offered him hospitality, shelter or support, and called for the burning of his books. For the rest of his life, Luther would live without legal protection. It would be very difficult – indeed, generally impossible – for him to travel outside the territories of Electoral Saxony.

The Wartburg and Reformation in Wittenberg

Luther had been instructed by the ban not to preach. However, on his return journey from Worms to Wittenberg, he found himself being invited – or even forced – to do so. In Hersfeld, he was welcomed by the abbot and by the town council, and made to preach, although he warned them that the town might thereby lose its imperial privileges. Travelling on to Eisenach, he again received a hearty welcome, and was asked to give a sermon. He reported that "the timid incumbent [of the parish] protested before me in the presence of a notary and witnesses, although he humbly apologised for having to do this through fear of his tyrants". Luther then went on to visit relatives. He was apprehended by Frederick the Wise's soldiers and carried off to the Wartburg, Frederick's castle near Eisenach. This abduction, which Luther almost certainly knew was going to happen, was intended to keep him safe in the aftermath of the Edict of Worms.

Luther remained in the Wartburg for nearly a year, abandoning his monk's tonsure by growing his hair and his beard, and passing as a knight. He wrote a treatise *On Monastic Vows*, and another, *Against Latomus*, exploring the relationship between justification by faith and the Holy Spirit. He published expositions of the Gospels and Epistles, as well as collections of model sermons on the readings set for Advent and Christmas, the "Advent and Christmas Postils". Most importantly, he worked on his translation of the New Testament into German, which would be published in September 1522. The "September Testament", as it came to be known, drew on Erasmus's edition of the New Testament, which Luther had known since it appeared in 1516. This was the beginning of Luther's work of Bible translation, perhaps his most significant and best known legacy, both for the theological accents which he set in his translation, and also for its influence on the development of the German language.

Frederick had ensured Luther's safety, but Luther's absence in Wittenberg left a vacuum into which Andreas Bodenstein von Karlstadt stepped. Karlstadt had been influenced by Staupitz and Luther to move away from his Thomist education to embrace a biblical theology, and had disputed with Johannes Eck in Leipzig on the subject of free will. Immediately after Luther's appearance and condemnation at the Diet of Worms he, together with the Wittenberg humanists Martin Reinhardt and Matthias Gabler, had been invited by King Christian II of Denmark to Copenhagen to teach Luther's ideas there. Considerable unrest had ensued, due largely to the unpopularity of the king, and Karlstadt left after only a month, leaving Gabler and Reinhardt to continue the work in Denmark as best they could. Back in Wittenberg, Karlstadt worked with Melanchthon and the town council to introduce church reforms based on Luther's teachings. Luther's monastery was the first to take concrete steps under the leadership of one of Luther's brother-friars, Gabriel Zwilling. On 29 September, the traditional celebration of the mass was discontinued and a simplified version substituted, still in Latin. Luther wrote a treatise on *The Misuse of the Mass* in support of this development. Additionally, Zwilling began to remove images from the church.

Karlstadt, supported by Zwilling and to some extent by his – and Luther's – university colleagues, Philip Melanchthon and Justus Jonas, sought to extend these reforms to the town church. Melanchthon published the first edition of his *Loci Communes*, or *Commonplaces*, a theological work which was the first systematic presentation of Luther's reforming theology. Karlstadt turned to more practical measures. On Christmas Day 1521, he conducted the service in Wittenberg's church in German instead of Latin, wearing his normal academic gown rather than ecclesiastical vestments, and encouraged the congregation to receive both bread and wine at communion. The same day, he announced his engagement to Anna von Mochau. They were married on 19 January, and Karlstadt thus demonstrated his rejection of the vow of celibacy he had taken on his ordination. By mid-January, Karlstadt had stopped hearing private confessions, had ceased to elevate the host during celebrations of the Eucharist, had rejected the rules about fasting, and was encouraging the removal of images and statues from Wittenberg's churches. Together with the city council, he worked to draft a church order for Wittenberg, dissolving confraternities and other lay orders, and setting up a poor chest to benefit from the proceeds of these dissolutions.

Matters were complicated by the presence in Wittenberg of a group of radical "prophets" who had been expelled from nearby Zwickau and been brought to Wittenberg by their leader, Thomas Müntzer. Müntzer and his followers were uncertain about the validity of infant baptism and they, like Karlstadt, believed that the Eucharist had a purely symbolic character. Their presence in Wittenberg made an already tense situation more difficult. Luther wrote to Melanchthon offering advice on how to test the authenticity of their words. Frederick, who despite his support for Luther was not enthusiastic about the evangelical theology, was already dismayed by the disorder in the Wittenberg church. He was even more horrified by the teachings of the Zwickau prophets and forbade any further changes in the Wittenberg churches.

Luther had long been of the opinion that actual practical reforms to the life of the church must have the agreement of the local rulers, both princes and magistrates. He felt that matters had moved too quickly in Wittenberg and, against Frederick's will, he left the Wartburg to return to Wittenberg at the beginning of March 1522 in response to the appeal of the town council. Donning his monk's habit, he preached a series of sermons recommending – for the sake of those with "weak consciences", who needed further teaching – the reversal of many of the changes which Karlstadt had introduced. He reinstated the mass in Latin, with reception of both bread and wine. Through this intervention Luther ensured that the

Reformation in Wittenberg would take an orderly, steady (some said over-cautious) course, rather than introducing sudden change.

In 1523, Luther produced a series of works relating to the proper conduct of worship in church, including a simplified *Formula of Mass and Communion for the Church at Wittenberg*, still in Latin, and a German baptismal liturgy which retained many of the baptismal rituals of the medieval rite, including exorcism, anointing, and clothing the child in white. Further liturgical reform would prove impossible until after Frederick's death in 1525, when his successor, his brother John, showed himself much more sympathetic to changes in the traditional liturgical rites and devotional practices of the church.

Luther turned to the writing of hymns intended to introduce congregations to the new theology. In 1524 he published a hymn book which included more than twenty of the forty hymns he would compose in the course of his career, although not yet "A Mighty Fortress is our God", which he wrote in 1529. Luther understood music and singing as gifts of God, which were rightly used in praising God and proclaiming God's saving work of grace. His hymns became one of the central means of spreading his theology to a population of which a significant proportion was illiterate. Along with his hymns went an appreciation of the importance of more formal education. Under Melanchthon's influence, Luther began to encourage the improvement of schools and education, writing in 1524 to remind city councils of their responsibilities to establish and sustain Christian education. Melanchthon's continuing efforts towards the reform of schools and universities were to earn him the title "Educator of Germany" – *Praeceptor Germaniae* – during his own lifetime.

Both Luther and Melanchthon realised that if the Reformation were to spread, preachers and teachers were needed who had been educated to read the Gospel in ways that were consistent with Luther's theology.

Defining the Reformation

The events in Wittenberg during the winter of 1521–22 had made it clear that Luther's message meant different things to different people. As his ideas spread, it became increasingly important to Luther to define his theology more precisely, show how it was rooted in a correct reading of Scripture, and establish what practices and actions were consistent with it. Luther was never a systematic thinker and was not above changing his arguments to counter whatever was being presented by his current opponents. Nonetheless, the closer definition of his theology was to be fundamental to much of what Luther wrote and did for the rest of his life. The period from 1524 until 1530 was marked by controversy and debates, some of which would split the emerging Protestant movement.

The Zwickau prophets had read Scripture and trusted in the direct inspiration of the Holy Spirit in ways which Luther found arbitrary and unconvincing, not least because they seemed to introduce an ethical rigour which was too close to the theology of works which he had so firmly rejected. After his expulsion from Wittenberg in 1522, Müntzer's convictions about Christian freedom and equality had led him to espouse the cause of the farmers and peasants who were protesting at their lack of political representation and the erosion of such freedoms as they had. These farmers' wars – *Bauernkriege,* as they are usually described in German (a better description than the English "peasants' war", since many of those involved were not peasants but educated, independent farmers seeking political representation) – had arisen at various places across the German lands from the end of the fifteenth century, but they took on new urgency in the mid-1520s as a result of some of the legal reforms in the empire. Müntzer became a leader of the farmers in Thuringia, and in September 1524 was the main author of the Mühlhausen Articles, which called for the dissolution of the town council and the formation of an "eternal council" based on divine justice and the Word of God. He was executed after the disastrous defeat at the battle of Mühlhausen in 1525.

Luther's first reaction to the growing unrest in that year was a treatise admonishing both rulers and farmers to peace, and pointing to their failures to take seriously the responsibilities and duties of their respective estates. However, when he realized that the actions and arguments of the farmers were being attributed to the influence of his theology, and that the resulting social unrest was being blamed on the Reformation, he was incensed. His treatise *Against the Murderous and Thieving Hordes of Farmers* was a heated and intemperate attack. It was unfortunate that its publication coincided with the massacre of a large group of rebels by the princes. It placed Luther firmly on the side of the already existent social order, and particularly of the princes and magistrates. Luther's reading of the Gospel might do away with the distinction between the spiritual and the temporal realms, but it did not make for a radical reordering of society.

This was also the year in which Luther's conflict with Erasmus came to a head. Their differences centred on the question of whether or not the human will could play a part in choosing salvation. Erasmus, like Luther, was deeply – and wittily – critical of the extravagant lifestyle of some bishops and abbots, of the bickering between monastic orders, and of the abuse of relics, pilgrimages, indulgences, fasting, monastic vows, and the invocation of saints. His satirical *In Praise of Folly* (1509) was widely read and highly influential. His editions of the Church Fathers made their thought accessible to the theologians of the sixteenth century; and his revised Latin translation of the New Testament with an edition of the Greek text (first edition printed in 1516) offered a basis for the critique of late-medieval theology as well as the new vernacular translations. Their contemporaries initially saw Luther as simply developing the ideas which Erasmus had begun. Erasmus, it was said, laid the egg which Luther had hatched. Erasmus himself disagreed with this analysis, commenting, "I laid a hen's egg: Luther hatched a bird of quite different breed."

Erasmus had become increasingly disturbed by several aspects of Luther's theology: his understanding of the interpretation of Scripture, which in Erasmus's view was over-simplistic; his rejection of the authority of the church and tradition, which in Erasmus's opinion raised more questions of authority than it answered; and his views on human nature, which ran contrary to Erasmus's understanding of the value of human will and reason. Erasmus was particularly concerned that Luther's approach would end by splitting the church rather than reforming it.

In autumn 1524 Erasmus published a treatise *On Free Will*, in which he presented his case, both biblical and theological, for the cooperation of the human free will in salvation. Luther did not respond immediately. He may have been reluctant to enter into disagreement with Erasmus, but he was also taken up with his concerns about the spreading social unrest across the German lands. In Wittenberg, he was coping with the aftermath of the death of Frederick the Wise in May, and in June his personal life changed when he married the former nun Katharina von Bora. He finally responded in late 1525 with *On Bound Will*, a swingeing attack on Erasmus in which Luther presented predestination to election as the inevitable consequence of the doctrine of justification by faith, and recommended that Erasmus restrict himself to his excellent work of producing good editions of texts rather than meddling with theology.

Erasmus was deeply hurt by Luther's failure to engage with his arguments and responded with two monumental treatises. He was also infuriated by the continued association of his own ideas with those of Luther's. As he had feared, "Erasmian" and "Lutheran" came to be used as synonymous terms of opprobrium by opponents of reform, including those who implemented the Inquisition in both Spain and Italy. This association was in part a recognition that Erasmus's influence on many reformers, including particularly Philip Melanchthon, Huldrych Zwingli, and John Calvin, was considerable. It reflected also a growing suspicion of Erasmus's work in conservative reforming circles within the Roman church. Erasmus died in 1536, five years before his works were placed on the Index of Forbidden Books in Rome. His attempts to distance himself from the Reformation had failed.

As early as 1520, Luther had redefined the number and meaning of the sacraments in opposition to medieval theology. The conflict with Karlstadt and Müntzer had shown, however, that his understanding of baptism and the Eucharist were not shared by all those who sought reform. By 1524, Huldrych

Zwingli, reformer in Zürich, had begun to articulate a theology of the Eucharist which Luther immediately associated with that of Karlstadt. The Eucharist was a memorial meal, a thanksgiving for the work of salvation done by Christ on the cross, and a bringing together of the people of God at which Christ was spiritually present. The bread and wine symbolized Christ's presence in the hearts of believers. For Zwingli they did not actually become Christ's body and blood. Moreover, and with some justification, Zwingli was convinced from his reading of Augustine that this was how the Eucharist had been understood in the early church.

In 1526, Luther wrote a treatise condemning Karlstadt's views on the Eucharist: *The Sacrament of the Body and Blood of Christ, Against the Fanatics.* Zwingli responded immediately with an explication of his own position, *A Short Teaching About the Lord's Supper*, followed the next year by his *Friendly Exegesis* in which he laid out his problems with Luther's position. Luther shot back a treatise affirming *That These Words "This is my body" Still Stand Fast*, to which Zwingli replied, *That These Words "This is my body" Will Always Have Their Old Meaning.* As the battle between Luther and Zwingli continued, theologians in Wittenberg and north Germany ranged themselves against those in south Germany and Switzerland. The theological controversy threatened to split the fledgling reform movement at a moment when its political unity had become desperately important.

Reform and Reformation in the German Empire

Luther's ideas had gained wide popular acclaim even by 1521, but the extent to which acceptance of his ideas led to changes in ecclesiastical practices and church structures was dependent on a range of factors. Political as well as religious interest was crucial, and personal contacts were important if the Reformation were to be "introduced". The introduction of the Reformation into a city or town usually involved a shift to vernacular liturgy, the administration of communion in the form of both bread and wine, the encouragement of vernacular preaching, the abandonment of distinctive forms of clerical dress, clergy receiving permission to marry, and the rejection of the authority of the local bishop. The closure of monasteries and convents, the setting up of a poor chest, and the diversion of ecclesiastical funds to support the poor or to pay for local needs (such as the repairing of roads and bridges) was often an associated step. These measures were usually initiated or authorized by the local prince and city council.

In 1517, Wenzelaus Linck, Dean of Wittenberg's Theology Faculty, was sent to Nuremberg as the Augustinian preacher. There he made Luther's ideas both known and popular. When in 1521 two of Nuremberg's prominent citizens, Willibald Pirckheimer and Lazarus Spengler, spoke out in favour of Luther's writings and were censured by the church authorities, the city council moved – not entirely successfully – to protect them. The way was paved for Nuremberg to become an early convert to the Reformation, but although by 1523 some priests had married, the Eucharist was being offered in both kinds, and the poor chest had been introduced, there had been no formal acceptance of the Reformation by the city council. The situation was similar in Strasbourg, although there the poor chest was not introduced until after the formal adoption of the German mass in 1524; and also in Ulm, where a majority of citizens seems to have accepted the teachings of either

Luther or Zwingli while continuing to attend the Latin mass. In Wittenberg, the full practical consequences of Luther's theology were eventually introduced only after the death of Frederick the Wise. Luther's "German Mass" did not appear until late 1525, or even early 1526.

Some towns and parishes, however, had moved to ban the Latin mass as the first step towards reform. In 1522, not long after Karlstadt's abortive attempts at sustained reform in Wittenberg the previous Christmas, a German evangelical mass was introduced in Nördlingen, in southern Germany, by Kaspar Keutz. In 1524 the mass started to be celebrated in German at Worms as well as at Strasbourg, and Müntzer also introduced a German evangelical mass in Alstadt. As discussed above, however, Müntzer's theological stance went far beyond what Luther considered reasonable. The introduction of vernacular liturgy or other reforms did not always imply acceptance of Luther's theology, although it did usually indicate an interest in biblical reform. In Lavonia (now Latvia), enthusiasm for the new teachings was accompanied by a frenzy of destruction of images which was far from the kind of orderly reform which Luther favoured. The young Philip of Hesse, who in 1524 was the first of the German princes to introduce the Reformation into his territory, was more attracted by the principle of *sola scriptura* than by the doctrine of justification by faith alone, and he also found Zwingli's theology of the Eucharist more convincing than Luther's.

The introduction of the Reformation therefore took different forms and had different theological accents depending on its context, on local interests and on the people involved. At the same time, the reforms shared common features. Many priests marked their conversion to evangelical beliefs by marrying, and the employment of married clergy by secular authorities, together with their protection against the measures meted out by the ecclesiastical authorities, could be an important step in the introduction of the Reformation. The reform of the liturgy, the use of the vernacular, the offering of communion in both kinds, the removal of the confessional: all of these were practical changes which marked reform. The closure of monasteries and convents, or the forced removal of the daughters who had been dedicated to the religious life was also common. Luther encouraged his congregations to sing, but more radical reform, such as that in Zürich, involved the removal of organs from churches. Zürich, like much of the Swiss confederation, Latvia, and later England, saw the destruction of images as part of the Reformation, a step against which Luther protested, since he felt it assigned to the images a power and significance that they did not have. There were similarities across the reforms. However, the theological disagreements over the Eucharist, different attitudes towards images, and varying approaches to church discipline would soon prove to present insurmountable obstacles between groups of Protestants.

Territories and imperial cities within the empire which took steps to introduce the Reformation were making a common political statement. They defied the Edict of Worms, and this gave them a political commonality against which other German rulers could and did react. In 1524, a synod of southern German rulers and bishops met in Regensburg to agree how to work against the new teachings while introducing reforms into the church. A year later, Duke George, Frederick and John's cousin, organized a union of north German rulers against the demands of the farmers and Luther's teachings. In response, the following year, Philip of Hesse and John of Saxony, Frederick the Wise's heir, entered into the Treaty of Gotha-Torgau. They were joined by the rulers of a number of other north German states and cities, including Brunswick, Anhalt, Mansfeld, and Magdeburg. John also signed a treaty with Prussia.

In 1526, the German rulers came together for an Imperial Diet at Speyer. The emperor was at war with France and at odds with Rome, in a conflict which would end with the Sack of Rome in May 1527. He therefore needed all the military support he could raise. Rather than reinforcing the Edict of Worms, as some of the more traditional princes had hoped, at Speyer an Edict of Toleration was passed, which declared of the princes and magistrates that "all so shall behave themselves in their several provinces as that they may be able to render an account of their doings both to God and the Emperor". Effectively, this allowed each ruler to determine the religious allegiance of their territory until a council of all the bishops of the church could be called, and it created a semi-legal space for the Reformation to expand.

By 1529, the political situation had changed. The emperor was enjoying a brief period of peace with France and could turn his attention to matters within the empire. The Imperial Diet met that year, again in Speyer. This Diet revoked the Edict of Toleration and called again for a council to establish unity in religion, declaring that in the meantime those who had held to the Edict of Worms should continue to do so, affirming that where changes had been introduced they might be retained but that no new changes should be allowed, instructing that the Latin mass be allowed everywhere, and forbidding all groups who denied the presence of Christ in the Eucharist or who rejected infant baptism. The Gospel, it maintained, should be preached "according to the teachings of the Church".

The Diet's decision provoked a Protest from fourteen imperial cities (Nuremberg, Strasbourg, Ulm, Constance, Rentlingen, Windsheim, Lindau, Kempten, Memmingen, Nordlingen, Heilbronn, Isny, St Gall, and Weissenburg; Frankfurt and Cologne, which initially joined the Protest, withdrew their signatures to the document before it was published) and five territories (Electoral Saxony, Hesse, Brandenburg, Lüneburg, and Anhalt). Drafted with the support and advice of several leading theologians, including Philip Melanchthon from Wittenberg, Simon Grynaeus from Basel, and Erhard Schnepf, who was Philip of Hesse's court preacher, the Protest complained that its signatories were being asked "to deny our Lord Jesus Christ, to reject His Holy Word"; and that it was necessary to "agree on what is meant by the true and holy Church". The Protest was presented to the Diet but was ignored. In frustration at the failure to listen to their concerns, the protesting rulers – from now on known as "Protestants" – met together to draw up a treaty, pledging their support for one another. But when representatives from Zürich indicated that they too would like to join, Wittenberg drew back, protesting that Zwingli's theology was not in line with Luther's.

This was a disaster for the political unity of the Protestants. Philip of Hesse was acutely aware of the strategic advantage of including Zürich in the treaty. He invited Luther and Zwingli to a meeting at his castle in Marburg to settle their differences. In October Luther and Zwingli met there, each bringing a group of supporters. Although the assembled theologians signed a list of fourteen points on which they agreed, they failed to agree about whether the body and blood of Christ were present in the bread and wine in the Eucharist. This was the result of underlying differences which Luther recognized: "You have a different mind!" he is said to have told Zwingli and his supporters. After Marburg, the Protestants found themselves in two camps, with Luther, Wittenberg and many of the German territories and cities on one side, and Zwingli in Zürich, together with the other Swiss cities and, at least initially, Martin Bucer in Strasbourg, on the other.

In the years that followed, Martin Bucer, Philip Melanchthon, and John Calvin would seek to resolve these differences, with little to show for their efforts. The Lutherans and the Reformed (as the reformers of Switzerland and the Rhineland came to be known) developed into separate confessions who did not receive the Eucharist from each other. It was not until 1973, with the signing of the Leuenberg Agreement, that Lutherans and the Reformed in Germany and Switzerland entered into a formal theological relationship which allowed them to share the Eucharist.

The Diet of Augsburg and the Augsburg Confession

Relationships between the Protestant princes and territories and the emperor continued to deteriorate, and in June 1530, a further Imperial Diet was convened at Augsburg. The emperor had two priorities: gaining support from the German princes to help him ward off the attacks of the Turks, who had besieged Vienna during September and October of the previous year and were still in possession of substantial areas of his territories in Hungary; and solving the religious tensions within the empire. To this end, he requested the major protagonists to draw up statements of faith and present them at the Diet. Luther could not attend, and had to stay in Coburg, more than 150 miles away. Philip Melanchthon was charged with presenting Wittenberg's statement, and probably drafted it. This was the *Confessio Augustana*, or *Augsburg Confession*, which reflected Luther's and Melanchthon's practical experience of introducing the Reformation into Saxony after 1525, as well as their theological insights. It would come to define the confessional basis of Lutheranism. A group of traditional theologians was invited to respond to it. They produced the *Papal Confutation*, or *Confutatio Pontificia*, which was read to the assembly by the emperor himself. Melanchthon responded with the *Apology*, or *Apologia*, a defence of the Augsburg Confession. Martin Bucer also presented a statement of faith, the *Confession of the Four Cities*, or *Confessio tetrapolitana*, on behalf of Strasbourg, Memmingen, Lindau and Constance, and Zwingli his *Account of the Faith*, or *Ratio Fidei*.

None of the Protestant statements was accepted by the emperor, and relationships deteriorated still further. Early in 1531, under the leadership of John of Saxony and Philip of Hesse, the Protestant princes and territories formed themselves into the Schmalkaldic League, a defensive alliance in case the emperor should take military steps against its members. In 1535 it was agreed that membership of the League should be open to those who subscribed to the Augsburg Confession. The Augsburg Confession thus became a defining statement of what it was to be Lutheran. Melanchthon adapted it in 1540 to make it more acceptable to the Swiss, producing the so-called *variata* version, but in 1555, nine years after Luther's death, and following nearly a decade of conflict within the empire, it was the original Augsburg Confession that became the basis for the Peace of Augsburg, making it legal for princes who subscribed to the Confession to use it as the definition of the church in their territories. Other theological positions, including those of Heinrich Bullinger in Zürich and John Calvin in Geneva, were not recognized in the empire until the end of the Thirty Years' War in 1648. Luther's theology, as interpreted by Melanchthon, thus defined and was defined by the process of official recognition of the Reformation in the German Empire.

CHAPTER 2

LUTHER'S THEOLOGY

Luther himself was sceptical about the wisdom of seeking to summarize his theological insights. In the preface to a collection of his German works published in Wittenberg in 1539, he remarked, "I would have been quite content to see my books, one and all, remain in obscurity and be consigned to oblivion." He also exhorted his readers not to concentrate on his own works, but on the Bible: "You should know that the Holy Scriptures constitute a book which turns the wisdom of all other books into foolishness, because not one teaches about eternal life except this one alone." For Luther, true theology had to be based on a proper understanding of the Scriptures, and this meant reading the Bible prayerfully. "Kneel down in your little room," he exhorted, "and pray to God with real humility and earnestness, that he through his dear Son may give you his Holy Spirit, who will enlighten you, lead you, and give you understanding." That enlightenment could be helped by reading the words of Scripture, not only in silence, but aloud, not only once, but over and over again, "repeating and comparing the spoken word and the written words of the book, reading and rereading them with diligent attention and reflection, so that you may see what the Holy Spirit means by them". It also meant understanding the realities of despair and temptation which led away from God. These experiences of despair and temptation – *tentatio*, or *Anfechtung*, as Luther called them – were for him "the touchstone which teaches you not only to know and understand, but also to experience how right, how true, how sweet, how lovely, how mighty, how comforting God's Word is, wisdom beyond all wisdom". What was important to Luther was the direct, personal experience of God, not reading about what someone else had thought or believed. Consequently, Luther also emphasized that his own writings should never lead other people to neglect to engage properly with the Word of God.

Luther was aware that he was not a systematic writer. In his introduction to his collected works in Latin, written the year before he died, he commented that because they had been written in response to events, his works were "crude and disordered chaos, which is now not easy to arrange even for me". Instead, he recommended more systematic works, such as that written by his friend and colleague Philip Melanchthon, as an aid to reading Scripture:

By God's grace a great many systematic books now exist, among which the *Loci Communes* of Philip excel, with which a theologian and a bishop can be beautifully and abundantly prepared to be mighty in preaching the doctrine of piety, especially since the Holy Bible itself can now be had in nearly every language.

Readers of his own works, Luther commented, should be aware that he had once been a monk and "a most enthusiastic papist", who in his earlier writings had conceded points "which I later and now hold and execrate as the worst blasphemies and abomination". Understanding Luther's theology and the themes he himself discovered in his reading and rereading of Scripture therefore means tracking his theological development and the shifts in his thought which formed and shaped his ideas.

Penitence, grace, and justification by faith

Luther is best known for his teaching of justification by faith through grace alone. He rejected the idea that a person's works could influence the way that God thought about them. However, he came to his conviction that a person's faith is all they need for salvation only after a long struggle.

Luther's anxieties about his own salvation had made him an assiduous monk who sought to gain God's favour. Long after he had left the order, defending himself against attacks from Duke George and other opponents in 1533, he reflected, "I was indeed a good monk and kept the rules of my order so strictly that I can say, if any monk ever got to heaven through monasticism, I would have done." At about the same time, in his lectures on Galatians, he remembered that when he had been a monk, he had tried hard to live according to the requirements of the monastic rule:

> I went to confession frequently, and I performed the assigned penances faithfully. Nevertheless, my conscience could never achieve certainty but was always in doubt. ... The longer I

tried to heal my uncertain, weak, and troubled conscience
with human traditions, the more uncertain, weak, and
troubled I continually made it.

As a monk, Luther's conscience was troubled, but he also
suffered on account of his sense that God was an oppressive,
terrifying judge. Writing in 1518 in defence of his Ninety-Five
Theses, he claimed that he "knew a man" whose experience of
God was of terrible judgment: "Then God appears horrifyingly
angry and with him the whole creation. There can be no
flight, no consolation either from within or without: all is
accusation." This "horror of despair", as Luther described it,
almost certainly reflected his own experience. It was from the
utter terror of being condemned by God that Luther sought
to be rescued.

Luther was helped through his crisis by Johann von Staupitz,
the Vicar-General of the reforming branch of the Augustinian
order to which Luther belonged. Staupitz was Professor for
Bible at Wittenberg (although he had little time to devote
to his lectures), and also Luther's confessor. It was Staupitz,
Luther affirmed, who taught him that he had misunderstood
God's righteousness. The cross was not about judgment, but
about mercy. Penitence was not about self-discipline and self-
denial but about love of God. Sending his Ninety-Five Theses
to Staupitz towards the end of May in 1518, Luther credited
Staupitz with turning his attention to reading the Scriptures:
"Your words on the subject of repentance pierced me like the
sharp arrows of power (Psalm 120:4 [VULGATE]), so that I
began to see what the Scriptures had to say about penitence."
What Luther found changed his understanding: "The texts
were so much in support of and favourable to your teaching

that although there had scarcely been any word in the Bible more bitter to me than 'penitence', ... now no word sounds sweeter or more pleasant to me than that." Luther was coming to realize that faith in God must be experienced and lived through understanding what Christ had done on the cross: "The commands of God become sweet when we understand that they are not to be read in books only, but in the wounds of the sweetest Saviour," he wrote in the same letter. By 1518, Luther had come to believe that Christ's work on the cross was the key to understanding salvation. A true theologian, he argued at the Heidelberg Disputation in spring of that year, was one "who comprehends the visible and manifest things of God revealed through suffering and the cross" (Thesis 20). Luther's was a "theology of the cross" (or, in Latin, *theologia crucis*), which understood God to work through suffering, and not a theology of glory, which understood God to work only through success.

Luther's appreciation of the understanding of God's merciful grace which he learnt from Staupitz was confirmed by what he read in the works of Augustine and further strengthened by his study of Greek and Hebrew. Luther's teachers had been influenced by humanist scholars such as Lorenzo Valla, Jacques Lefèvre d'Étaples (known in Latin as Faber Stapulensis), whose *Commentary on Romans* Luther knew and valued, and Erasmus, who did important work in editing the works of Augustine and other Church Fathers and who in 1516 would publish a corrected Latin translation of the New Testament with Greek text which would become the foundation of Luther's German translation of the New Testament. Through his reading of Lefèvre and Erasmus Luther learnt that the Vulgate, the standard Latin translation of Scripture used during the Middle Ages, contained a number of problematic translations which changed the sense of the original Greek and Hebrew texts. In Matthew's Gospel (4:17), Christ exhorted his followers to "Repent" and not, as the Vulgate had it to "Do penance". The Greek verb used, *metanoiete*, as Luther noted in his defence of the Ninety-Five Theses, was derived from the Greek words for "afterwards" (*meta*) and "mind" (*nous*), "so that penitence or *metanoia* is 'coming to one's right mind, afterwards', that is, comprehension of your own evil after you have found out your error".

Luther came to believe that repentance must mean both the change of mind and the means by which that change came about, that is the grace of God. This idea was central to the first of his Ninety-Five Theses: "When our Lord and Master Jesus Christ said, 'Repent', he willed the entire life of believers to be one of repentance." Luther believed that the Vulgate's translation "Do penance" had been wrongly used to justify the complex systems which had grown up around the process of confessing and being granted remission of sins. Instead of repenting and amending their lives, people had been led to believe that they could attain the same benefit by paying for prayers or celebrations of the mass to be said for them, or by buying letters of indulgence or other exemptions from various aspects of Canon Law such as the Lenten fast. "Christians are to be taught that he who gives to the poor or lends to the needy does a better deed than he who buys indulgences," he insisted in his Ninety-Five Theses. Real contrition was necessary, and that would manifest itself in works of love through which, he could still suggest at this stage, "love would grow and the person become better". However, by the time of the Heidelberg Disputation, he was insisting that if done for the wrong reason – to try to win God's favour – even works of love could be sinful: "Human works always seem attractive and good, but they are nevertheless likely to be mortal sins." It was faith which was important for salvation, and not works, even works of love. "The law says, 'do this,' and it is never done," he concluded at Heidelberg. "Grace says, 'believe in this,' and everything is already done." This realization was an important step in the development of Luther's doctrine of justification by faith alone.

Luther worked out his ideas about justification over a period of several years, first through his lectures on the Psalms and on Paul's letter to the Romans, none of which was published in his lifetime, and then in the course of the controversy which followed the issuing of his Ninety-Five Theses on 31 October 1517. His lectures on the Psalms (1513–15) show him reading them as prophecies of Christ, to be interpreted by reference to other biblical texts. From the beginning of his lectures, Luther was engaging with the questions of judgment, grace, free will, and law which were to shape his theology. Characteristic themes of humility and repentance, which would prove foundational to his doctrine of justification by faith, emerged as he expounded the Psalms (which, as a monk, he prayed every day). At this stage these themes were still related to an understanding of judgment which saw it in terms of a self-accusation which leads to a knowledge of Christ: "'Judgment' [*iudicium*]," Luther commented in his notes on Psalm 1,

> is the sentence of condemnation. It properly involves a
> man's accusing, detesting, and condemning himself, as
> our theologians talk about the acts of penitence. ... It is
> impossible for one who confesses his sin not to be righteous
> [iustus], for he speaks the truth, and where the truth is, there
> is Christ.

By the time he reached Psalm 71 (Psalm 70 in his original numbering), Luther had begun to see that one consequence of this is that trust must be placed in God. To place hope in God is to abandon hope in the world:

> No-one can say "And save me," except one who understands and acknowledges himself to be weak and sick and condemned. Therefore those who consider themselves saved and who are pleased with their own health in the flesh, in the world, and in riches do not pray, even if they have uttered these words.

Luther could not yet say, as he later would, that the Law exists to convince those who discover that they cannot keep it of their sinfulness, but he was deeply aware of the need for both penitence and trust in God.

In his commentary on Psalm 71, Luther also expressed his growing conviction that sin remained a continuing reality even after grace had been received. "Even when the soul has been delivered through righteousness," he wrote, "we are still held through the body in the dangers and the captivity and exile of this life." There was already a hint here that Luther's understanding of justification would go beyond that of Augustine, seeing justification not as something given or imparted to the sinner, making the sinner intrinsically less sinful, but as something reckoned or imputed to the sinner, according to which the sinner's guilt would not be counted against them, but they would not actually change.

By the time he came to lecture on Paul's letter to the Romans (1515–16), Luther had reflected further on this question and come to understand God's righteousness in a new way. "We must be taught a righteousness that comes completely from the outside and is alien", he explained in his introduction to his lectures. In his commentary on Romans 1:17, "the righteousness of God is revealed", Luther noted: "By the righteousness of God we must not understand the righteousness by which He is righteous in Himself but the righteousness by which we are made righteous by God." Luther was convinced that understood in this way "the righteousness of God is the cause of salvation". This was not something that human beings could do for themselves. Instead, people needed to realize and acknowledge their inability to overcome their sinful state: "[God] Himself makes us righteous when we confess that we cannot overcome our sin. He does this, when we believe His words; for through such believing He justifies us; that is, He accounts us as righteous." Righteousness in a scriptural sense, Luther concluded, is not "a quality of the soul". Rather, "We are all born in iniquity, that is, in unrighteousness, and we die in it, and we are righteous only by the accounting of a merciful God through faith in His Word."

For Luther, this was the central realization: God did not use his Gospel to add punishment to punishment. Rather, as Luther wrote in an autobiographical note a year before his death:

> I began to understand that the righteousness of God is that
> by which the righteous lives by a gift of God, namely by faith.
> And this is the meaning: the righteousness of God is revealed
> by the gospel, namely, the passive righteousness with which
> merciful God justifies us by faith, as it is written, "He who
> through faith is righteous shall live." Here I felt that I was
> altogether born again and had entered paradise itself through
> open gates. There a totally other face of the entire Scripture

showed itself to me. Thereupon I ran through the Scriptures from memory. I also found in other terms an analogy, as, the work of God, that is, what God does in us, the power of God, with which he makes us strong, the wisdom of God, with which he makes us wise, the strength of God, the salvation of God, the glory of God.

Luther concluded from this recognition – often known as his "Reformation breakthrough" – that not only righteousness, but everything good, must come from God. Human beings must recognize themselves to be as nothing in comparison. He laid this out schematically in the notes for his lectures on Romans:

	wise	*unless we*	*foolish*
God in	*righteous*	*believe Him and*	*unrighteous*
His words	*truthful*	*submit to Him*	*liars*
cannot be	*strong*	*by confessing*	*weak*
	good	*that we are*	*evil*

Consequently, Luther argued, nothing that a person did out of their own intentions or their own strength could lead them towards God.

For Luther, the recognition that everything good must come from God was the central message of Paul's letter to the Romans, as he explained at the very beginning of his lectures: "The chief purpose of this letter is to break down, to pluck up, and to destroy all wisdom and righteousness of the flesh. This includes all the works which in the eyes of people or even in our own eyes may be great works." Since righteousness could only come from God, Luther concluded that works, even if they were apparently good, were in fact nothing of the kind, particularly if they were carried out with any intention of making a person righteous. He argued that those who believed

> that it was sufficient if they possessed virtue and knowledge, … even though they did not parade their righteousness before men and did not boast of it but followed it from a real love of virtue and wisdom, … could not refrain from being pleased with themselves in their innermost hearts and from glorying only in themselves – at least in their hearts – as righteous and good men.

Luther therefore rejected any such trust in the human ability to achieve righteousness. He was critical of the teaching of Aristotle, whose philosophy made up the mainstay of university studies in the late Middle Ages. Luther was especially opposed to the use of Aristotle's *Ethics*, which, he thought, taught people to trust in their own abilities to order their lives so as to achieve righteousness, and with it God's favour. Indulgences were, he thought, a symptom of a far deeper problem. People had come to rely for salvation, not on God, but on their own power to determine the good and do it.

In taking this position, Luther rejected a central tenet of late-medieval, scholastic understandings of justification. Writing on justification, the fifteenth-century theologian Gabriel Biel had argued, following William of Ockham (the father of the "nominalist" school of medieval philosophy, taught in German universities as the *via moderna*), that nothing anyone did could ever be enough to achieve righteousness in God's eyes. On the other hand, with Thomas Aquinas, the father of the so-called "realist" school, taught as the *via antiqua*, Biel argued that everyone must do all that they could, in the sure confidence that even though it could never be enough, a gracious God would count it as if it were.

In a disputation on free will held in 1516, Luther had already rejected the idea that God was bound to reward those who did all that they could, arguing that, on the contrary, this attitude added to sin. At the Heidelberg Disputation, he maintained that "the person who believes that he can obtain grace by doing what is in him adds sin to sin so that he becomes doubly guilty". Works counted for nothing in God's eyes. All that mattered was faith, and faith could accomplish everything.

Luther explored the implications of his conviction in *On the Freedom of a Christian*. Here he wrote that "true faith in Christ is a treasure beyond comparison, which brings with it complete salvation and saves man from every evil". Faith "makes the law and works unnecessary for anyone's righteousness and salvation", giving freedom from such demands. Through faith "we ascribe to God truthfulness, righteousness, and whatever else should be ascribed to one who is trusted" and in doing so, "the soul consents to his will". Picking up on his earlier thoughts on the meaning of justification, he explained that faith "unites the soul with Christ as a bride is united with her bridegroom" so that everything that was the soul's – sins, death, and damnation – is taken over by Christ, and all that is Christ's – grace, life, and salvation – becomes the soul's. Faith, Luther was convinced, set people free from the fruitless task of seeking to earn their salvation. This message caught the hearts of many who heard it.

Law and Gospel

Luther's doctrine of justification by faith taught that people were set free from the demands of works and of the Law. For Luther, this involved a radical reassessment of the theological role of the Law and its relationship to the Gospel. Luther came to believe that the Law, by which he meant primarily the Ten Commandments, was important not only because it showed people what they ought to be doing, but also because it convinced them that they could not do it. Filled with despair at that realization, they would turn to God and entreat him for the grace proclaimed by the Gospel.

In 1513, at the beginning of his lectures on the Psalms, Luther could still speak of the Gospel using the language of Law: "The Gospel is not the Law of Christ unless it be grasped by faith." The "rod of iron" described in Psalm 2 (verse 9: "You shall break them with a rod of iron, and dash them in pieces like a potter's vessel", NRSV) "is the holy Gospel, which is Christ's royal sceptre in His church and kingdom. ... It is called a 'rod' because it directs, convicts, reproves, and upholds, etc." The Gospel

> puts the misshapen in order, that is, it disciplines the undisciplined, it crushes the great (that is, it humbles the proud); it bends what stands erect (that is, it puts down the puffed up), it smoothes the rough places (that is, it calms down the angry), it lengthens the short (that is, it makes the fearful long-suffering); on the other hand, it cuts off the long (that is, it terrifies the presumptuous), it gets rid of rust (that is, it banishes sloth), etc.

At this stage, Luther concluded that "the Law of the Gospel is the truth without a covering". Discussing Psalm 76, he explained that those who had received the Gospel "were born of the Law, for they were begotten by the Word of God out of Holy Scripture". Luther was still thinking of the Gospel as in some way developing and completing the Law.

In the course of his lectures on Romans, Luther's ideas about the Law developed further. Commenting on Romans 2:13, he argued that "the doers of the Law will be justified", explaining that through justification people become doers of the Law, and "that they will be looked upon and thought of as righteous" – that is, counted as righteous. These true "doers of the Law", he suggested, must be those who keep the Law not only outwardly, but "with their will and their heart", and this was only possible once they were justified. Therefore, "doers of the Law" in this sense were actually doing works of faith or grace, which were "done out of the spirit of liberty and solely for the love of God". This was only possible for those who had been justified by faith. Luther still wanted to distinguish between different kinds of "doers of the Law": those who acted through faith and those who did only the external "works of the Law".

In his Romans lectures, Luther also used the term "works of the Law" to refer to works pleasing to God and contributing to righteousness. "Works of the Law," he suggested, are "those which are regarded in themselves as being sufficient for righteousness and salvation", through which the person who does them wills the grace of justification, "for a large part of righteousness is the will to be righteous". On this reading, the Gospel was the "new Law":

the old Law says to those who are proud in their own
righteousness: "You must have Christ and His Spirit"; the new
Law says to those who humbly admit their spiritual poverty
and seek Christ: "Behold, here is Christ and His Spirit."

Luther had not yet come to see Law and Gospel in pronounced
contrast to each other.

By the time he came to comment on Romans 10, however,
he was using language which was to become characteristic of
his later theology:

> For the Law shows nothing but our sin, makes us guilty,
> and thus produces an anguished conscience; but the Gospel
> supplies a longed for remedy to people in anguish of this
> kind. Therefore the Law is evil, and the Gospel good; the Law
> announces wrath, but the Gospel peace. The Law says (as the
> apostle cites in Galatians 3:10): "Cursed be everyone who does
> not abide by all things written in the book of the Law and
> do them." But no one continues in them to do them, as it is
> written in the same place: "For all who rely on works of the
> Law are under a curse." But the Gospel says: "Behold the Lamb
> of God, who takes away the sin of the world" (John 1:29). The
> Law oppresses the conscience with sins, but the Gospel frees
> the conscience and brings peace through faith in Christ.

In Luther's mature thought, Law and Gospel were distinct
because they had two entirely different functions. Discussing
Galatians 3:2 in the early 1530s, Luther concluded: "The Law
is a taskmaster; it demands that we work and that we give. In
short, it wants to have something from us. The Gospel, on the

contrary, does not demand; it grants freely; it commands us to hold out our hands and to receive what is being offered." In Luther's view, the Law made impossible demands, while the Gospel was a free gift.

This is not to say that Luther believed the Law to be of no use. On the contrary, he understood it to be of fundamental importance. For Luther, knowledge of sin came through the Law. Paul himself had written, "I would not have known what it is to covet if the Law had not said, 'You shall not covet'" (Romans 7:7, NRSV). Moreover, Luther was convinced that the Law was important because, as Augustine had pointed out, it was through the realization that they could not keep the Law that people of faith would learn to put their reliance on God:

> The people of the Law say to the Law and to God, who speaks in the Law: "I have done what you commanded; it is done as you ordered." But the people of faith say: "I cannot do; I have not done; but give me what you command; I have not done it, but I desire to do it. And because I cannot, I beg and beseech of you the power whereby I may do it." ... And thus there is a very real difference between these classes of people, because the one says: "I have done it," and the other says, "I beg that I might be empowered to do it."

Through the Law, thought Luther, people came to recognize their need for the grace which is preached in the Gospel. This is the theological use of the Law: the Law convicts the sinner of their sin. Luther also believed the Law to be important because of its political or civic use for maintaining order in society "to restrain those who are uncivilized and wicked"; this he often called the first use of the Law. However, in matters of justification it was the theological use of the Law which he saw as primary.

Writing against Erasmus in 1525, Luther related the distinction between Law and Gospel to the distinction between the Old and the New Testaments: "The New Testament properly consists of promises and exhortations, just as the Old Testament properly consists of laws and threats," he explained. He would later come to see the distinction between Law and Gospel as somewhat less obviously related to the distinction between Old and New Testament, and he always maintained that even in the Old Testament it was the Gospel, in Christ, and not the Law which saved. Paul, writing to the Galatians, did not insist that Titus be circumcised; for Luther, this was evidence, as he explained in his Galatians lectures, that "the patriarchs and all the Old Testament saints were free in their conscience and were justified by faith, not by circumcision or the Law". Luther could therefore affirm that "the patriarchs, prophets, and devout kings in the Old Testament were righteous, having received the Holy Spirit secretly on account of their faith in the coming Christ". Nonetheless, in Luther's understanding, Christ's coming meant that the Law was superseded, not that it was fulfilled.

The danger of Luther's theology of justification by faith, and particularly of his teaching about Law and the uselessness of good works for salvation, was – as his critics were quick to point out – that it could lead people to believe that they no longer needed to keep the Law. However, Luther's understanding of the relationship between Law and Gospel was not that the believer progressed from being "under the Law" to being "under the Gospel", but that they were simultaneously under both. He expressed this in terms of the paradox with which he opened *The Freedom of a Christian*: "A Christian is a perfectly free lord of all, subject to none. A Christian is a perfectly dutiful servant of all, subject to all." The affirmation that every person is at the same time both justified and a sinner – *simul iustus et peccator* – is fundamental to Luther's theology. Luther saw this idea expressed in Psalm 38 and Romans 7. In his lectures on Romans, he expounded Psalm 38:18, "I confess my iniquity. I am sorry for my sin", in these terms: "Therefore, wonderful and sweet is the mercy of God, who at the same time considers us both as sinners and non-sinners. Sin remains and at the same time it does not remain." Consequently, as he explained in a gloss (a textual comment) on Romans 7:25:

> as one and the same person I am at the same time spiritual and carnal, because with my mind, that is, with the inner man and spiritually, [I] serve the Law of God, that is, I do not lust, but rather I love God and the things of God, but with my flesh, in the outward man, I serve the law of sin, the tinder of sin and concupiscence, because I lust and I hate the things of God.

Luther's conviction that all people are *simul iustus et peccator* is closely linked with his belief that righteousness is not imparted but imputed. As he put it in his comments on Romans 4:7, to affirm that someone is "at the same time both a sinner and a righteous man" is to say that that person is "a sinner in fact, but righteous by the sure imputation and promise of God that he will continue to deliver him from sin until he has completely cured him".

Despite the concerns of his critics, Luther did not believe that his approach to justification meant that no one should do good works. His intention was to put an end to the idea that people could earn their salvation through their own actions. "Our faith in Christ does not free us from works but from false opinions concerning works, that is, from the foolish presumption that justification is acquired by works," he concluded in *On the Freedom of a Christian*. Certainly, his conviction that a person was *simul iustus et peccator* meant that people would be granted justification freely, but that did not mean that they could do whatever they desired. Luther believed that human desires, lusts and passions tended to lead away from faith. The "outer man", being still sinful, was subject to these temptations and needed to discipline them:

> In this life he must control his own body and have dealings with men. Here the works begin; here a man cannot enjoy leisure; here he must indeed take care to discipline his body by fastings, watchings, labours, and other reasonable discipline and to subject it to the Spirit so that it will obey and conform to the inner man and faith and not revolt against faith and hinder the inner man, as it is the nature of the body to do if it is not held in check.

For this reason, Luther could assert that every Christian, while free and justified before God, lives also in bondage, "a perfectly dutiful servant of all, subject to all". The traditional disciplines of ecclesiastical life – particularly fasting and praying – were therefore important, not as works which could earn God's favour, but as a means of controlling sinful distractions.

Luther also affirmed that faith would necessarily give rise to good works. Good works did not make someone good, but were the fruits of justification:

> Good works do not make a good man, but a good man does good works; evil works do not make a wicked man, but a wicked man does evil works, ... as Christ also says, "A good tree cannot bear evil fruit, nor can a bad tree bear good fruit" [Matthew 7:18].

The works of someone not justified, therefore, were necessarily evil: "If a man were not first a believer and a Christian, all his works would amount to nothing and would be truly wicked and damnable sins." Faith, on the other hand, would naturally emanate in good works, but these works would be works which were an expression of the deep love for God discovered in faith. They would not be actions defined or prescribed by the church, but works of service to neighbour without expectation of praise or reward.

Such good works are the completion of the message of the New Testament, as Luther would later maintain when writing against Erasmus. In the New Testament "the gospel is preached", the free offer of the Spirit and grace by God through Christ crucified; there follow

> exhortations, in order to stir up those who are already justified and have obtained mercy, so that they may be active in the fruits of the freely given righteousness and of the Spirit, and may exercise love by good works and bravely bear the cross and all other tribulations of the world.

In this sense the Gospel would and should bear fruit, as Luther explained in the final section of *The Freedom of a Christian*: "From faith thus flow forth love and joy in the Lord, and from love a joyful, willing, and free mind that serves one's neighbour willingly and takes no account of gratitude or ingratitude, of praise or blame, of gain or loss." A believer's joy in the Gospel and love of God would lead them to undertake works of selfless love.

Luther's teaching on Gospel freedom and the ineffectiveness of works clearly resonated with many people who had felt burdened by the need to earn their salvation. It inspired significant numbers of monks and nuns to leave their monasteries and convents. It offered a new source of inspiration to the farmers and peasants who were demanding political rights and freedoms. But it deeply worried some of the humanists who had seen Luther as espousing their cause. The most significant figure in this group was Erasmus.

Free will and works

Erasmus seems initially to have been quite favourable towards Luther. He wrote to Frederick the Wise in 1519 that, although he did not know Luther and had only read parts of his writings, he did not approve of the proceedings against him. At first sight, Luther's writings against scholastic theology and his polemic against indulgences and their abuse seemed in line with Erasmus's own critique of impiety and ecclesiastical excess, presented in a range of writings including the satirical and popular *In Praise of Folly* (1509). However, it soon became clear that Luther's theological convictions were driving him to call for reforms which were much more radical than those envisaged by Erasmus.

Erasmus believed that the key to reforming the church lay in providing people with the means to live proper Christian lives, informed by scholarly attitudes of mind. Two weapons are necessary for the Christian, he asserted in his *Handbook for the Christian Soldier*: prayer and knowledge. With the help of prayer it was possible to understand the true meaning of Scripture, which for Erasmus meant uncovering the "mysteries" behind the letter of Scripture, as had the Church Fathers Origen, Ambrose, Jerome, and Augustine in their commentaries on Paul. Scripture was important as a guide, but Erasmus also affirmed the value of classical scholarship as a guide to a godly life:

> If you take the best from the books of the pagans and follow
> the example of the bee in the garden of the ancients rejecting
> all that is poisonous and sucking in only the healing and
> noble nectar, then you will have gained much for the kind of
> common life which they call ethical.

Reason, for Erasmus, must be the ruling principle within human beings, guiding them towards the godly aspects of themselves, and thus making them more pleasing to God. For Erasmus, the decision to seek a closer relationship with God was, at least to some extent, the prerogative of a person's will. Erasmus was disturbed to discover from Luther's *Assertio* (1520) that Luther rejected the fundamental premises of Erasmus's theology, denying the reality of human freedom and asserting that everything that happens in matters of salvation is by absolute necessity.

Erasmus was initially reluctant to write against Luther, fearing that he would thereby give further ammunition to those who opposed the humanist approach to learning.

However, once Luther had been excommunicated and banned in 1521, Erasmus found himself being pressed by some of his more influential followers to distance himself from Luther's views. These followers included Adriaan Boeyens, a fellow Dutchman who was elected Pope Adrian VI on the death of Leo X in 1522, and several princes.

Erasmus's treatise *On Free Choice* (*de libero arbitrio*) was published in 1524. It began by pointing out that Luther had the authority of the Church Fathers against him. Erasmus explained that he would restrict his discussion to the opinion of Scripture on the question of free will, since this was the only authority that Luther accepted. However, he also emphasized that the question of how to determine the correct interpretation of Scripture remained unresolved, and expressed his unease at Luther's appeal to his own interpretative authority over that of many generations of commentators. Erasmus went on to present a series of passages in support of free choice, followed by others which opposed it. He concluded with an examination of Luther's arguments in the *Assertio*, and an epilogue in which he explained his own position.

For Erasmus, if there were no freedom of choice then there could be no merit. There could also be no sense in God's Law, for in his view the commandment "You shall ..." necessarily implied the ability to obey that command. If people could not choose whether or not they obeyed, then God's reward or punishment would be entirely arbitrary, and therefore unjust. But Erasmus did not believe that God was unjust, and therefore he believed that human beings must have the ability to exercise their will in matters of salvation.

However, Erasmus also believed that salvation was impossible without grace, and he was prepared to concede that the will could achieve nothing on its own. For him the human will's choice of salvation was like an infant who wants an apple from the other side of the room. The child wants the apple, but is incapable of reaching it on his own. He can only attain what he desires if his parent helps him across the room. The important point for Erasmus was that the child wants the apple in the first place. Similarly, human beings needed God's grace to aid their will since all the will can do is to make a very small contribution towards desiring God; it cannot actually achieve merit.

Erasmus thought that human beings could be said to cooperate in some sense with God in salvation, but that in this salvific cooperation "God's grace is the first cause, but human will is the second cause." For Erasmus, the existence of that element of human choice in desiring to cooperate with God rescued human beings from any form of determinism. This he regarded also as the teaching of the church over centuries and, despite his criticism of the church, he believed that it was the church that had authority to determine doctrine. "I will put up with this Church until I see a better one and it will have to put up with me until I become better."

Luther's delayed response, *On Bound Choice* (*De servo arbitrio*), finally appeared in late 1525. In it Luther laid out his objections to Erasmus's arguments. He asserted that the meaning of Scripture was clear and unambiguous, insisting that it demonstrated that the human will was not free to choose salvation. Erasmus's approach, Luther complained, entirely missed the point:

> He has no idea of making any distinction between the Old and the New Testament, for he sees almost nothing in either

except laws and precepts, by which men are to be trained in good manners. What the new birth is, however, or renewal, regeneration, and the whole work of the Spirit, of this he sees nothing at all.

Salvation, for Luther, represented a much more fundamental, radical change than living an ethically good life.

Luther wanted to distinguish between the exercise of free choice in matters of ethics or politics and its exercise in matters of salvation. He argued that with regard to "faculties and possessions" a person "has the right to use, to do, or to leave undone, according to his own free choice" – although even in these matters, God "acts in whatever way he pleases". But human free choice is

allowed to man only with respect to what is beneath him and not what is above him. … In relation to God, or in matters pertaining to salvation or damnation, a man has no free choice, but is a captive, subject and slave either of the will of God or the will of Satan.

Luther's conviction that the human will was not able to choose salvation was rooted in his understanding of the meaning of the crucifixion. Christ died to reconcile sinful human beings to God. If it were possible for the human will to exercise any element of choice for God, then that part of the will would be good in and of itself, and it would not have been necessary for Christ to die to redeem it: "What need is there of the Spirit or of Christ or of God if free choice can overcome the motions of the mind toward evil?"

He had been moving towards this position for some time. Theses 13 and 14 of the Heidelberg Disputation (1518) had denied the existence of free will after the fall of Adam and Eve:

> Free will, after the Fall, exists in name only, and as long as it does what it is able to do, it commits a mortal sin. Free will, after the Fall, has power to do good only in a passive capacity, but it can always do evil in an active capacity.

Since the fall, in Luther's view, the human will has been captive to sin, "not that it is nothing, but that it is not free except to do evil". This had been one of the points of criticism raised in the list of errors published in conjunction with the Bull *Exsurge Domine*. In his 1521 rebuttal of that list, Luther had asserted: "It is a profound and blind error to teach that the will is by nature free and can, without grace, turn to the spirit, seek grace, and desire it." Luther had come to believe that one consequence of asserting justification by faith alone was that not only grace, but also faith must be given to human beings by God. "We can do nothing of ourselves," he told Erasmus, and "whatever we do, God works it in us". It was God who decided who would be saved, and therefore it must be God who decided who was to have faith and granted it to them. This is the doctrine of predestination, which for Luther was a consequence of his strong emphasis on justification by faith.

One consequence for Luther was that God can, and does, will actions which appear to human beings to have evil consequences. Luther had begun to explore this idea in his Romans lectures, when he asserted: "This sentence is correct: God wills evil, or sins." This assertion, he explained, is not an assertion that God *is* evil in the way that human beings are evil, for "[evil] remains outside [God], and a creature commits it, either a man or a demon" – nonetheless, it must be realized that "if God did not want it to happen, it would not happen". In *On Bound Choice*, Luther explored how God's purposes are worked out by a God who "works life, death, and all in all":

> when God makes alive he does it by killing, when he justifies he does it by making men guilty, when he exalts to heaven he does it by bringing down to hell, as Scripture says: "The Lord kills and brings to life; he brings down to hell and raises up" [1 Samuel 2:6] … God hides his eternal goodness and mercy under eternal wrath, his righteousness under iniquity.

Luther saw these as the hidden ways in which God works, the ways of God hidden (*deus absconditus*), in contrast to the revelation of love found in the ways of God revealed (*deus revelatus*). They were shown most powerfully in Christ's death for humankind by which, as he put it in the Heidelberg Disputation, "visible and manifest things of God are seen through suffering and the cross". To know Christ was to know "God hidden in suffering". Luther believed that God worked in these hidden ways "in order that there may be room for faith". A proper appreciation of the consequences of bound choice offered one of the best opportunities for true faith: "This is the highest degree of faith, to believe [God] merciful when he saves so few and damns so many, and to believe him righteous when by his own will he makes us necessarily damnable."

Luther did not believe that an awareness of these matters would aid the faith of all believers. In his lectures on Romans, he concluded his discussion of the assertion that "God wills evil" with a comment that such questions were a matter only for theologians: "These statements contain the most subtle secrets of theology, such as ought not to be treated in the presence of simple and unlearned people but only among experts." Notably, his discussion of predestination, bound choice and the actions of the *deus absconditus* was largely restricted to the Latin works in which he dealt with the more technical theological questions. In his German works, which were generally more practical and catechetical, he painted a different, more encouraging picture, identifying God as the source of goodness. The *Large Catechism* made no mention of predestination or of the dark, hidden sides of God's work which Luther had asserted against Erasmus. Rather, the focus was on God as good and the source of all goodness. It is appropriate, Luther averred, that in German (as indeed in English) the word "God" (German, *Gott*) derives from the word "good" (German, *gut*), for God is "an eternal fountain which gushes forth abundantly nothing but what is good, and from which flows forth all that is and is called good". Consequently, he suggested:

> we are to trust in God alone, and look to Him and expect from Him naught but good, as from one who gives us body, life, food, drink, nourishment, health, protection, peace, and all necessaries of both temporal and eternal things. He also preserves us from misfortune, and if any evil befall us, delivers and rescues us, so that it is God alone (as has been sufficiently said) from whom we receive all good, and by whom we are delivered from all evil.

Trust in God, for Luther, was faith. In his vernacular teaching works he seemed to offer something of a corrective to what he had written to Erasmus, suggesting that faith is something – indeed the only thing – that human beings can usefully do.

The idea that faith is the only proper human work was found also in Luther's rejection of the benefit of other works. In 1520, in a treatise *On Good Works* (an exegesis of the Ten Commandments) dedicated to John of Saxony, Luther described faith quite explicitly as a work: "The first and highest, the most precious of all good works is faith in Christ." Faith, Luther suggested, understood as "faithfulness, confidence deep in the heart", is the true fulfilment of the first commandment that we should love God above all things; no other work is able to satisfy this commandment. He saw a significant difference between "keeping the First Commandment with outward works only, and keeping it with inward trust". Here Luther seemed to suggest that faith and trust are something that the believer has some control over.

Although he no longer spoke explicitly of faith as a work, the sense that believers should be active in trusting God and seeking to strengthen and sustain their faith also emerged from Luther's catechetical works, and especially his *Large Catechism*. Here Luther emphasized the need to have true faith and trust in God. Faith, he said, existed "when the heart lays hold of him and clings to him". Hearts, minds and lives must be constantly directed towards God, not in an attempt to gain salvation, but as a means to aid believers in their constant struggle against sin and the temptations of the body, which for Luther meant against the devil. Here active works of faith and of keeping the Ten Commandments were vital: "You will not find a stronger incense or other fumigation against the devil than by being engaged upon God's commandments and words, and speaking, singing, or thinking of them."

The *Large Catechism* indicated that Luther's conviction regarding the inability of the human will to choose God did not blind him to the need to encourage his followers to persevere in the faith and to cultivate habits of prayer and openness to God. Luther would no doubt have reminded his fellow theologians and students that in the end it would be God's decision as to whether faith was true, but people must nonetheless be encouraged to study Scripture, to pray, and to show their love of God through love of neighbour.

Sacraments

The sacraments were the axis about which the wheel of late-medieval church life turned. They were viewed as the primary means by which God gave grace through the church to his people. The medieval church taught that there were seven sacraments: baptism, which was administered to babies; confirmation, which was generally administered to children aged eight or older; the Eucharist or the mass, which people might attend often, but would receive seldom, and at which they would be offered only the bread; penance, the confession of sins to a priest who would then impose a penance and pronounce absolution; extreme unction or the last rites, the anointing of the sick shortly before death; ordination, which authorized those who received it to administer sacraments; and marriage. Confession and the mass were the focus of most people's regular contact with the sacramental life of the church, and both had become highly formalized.

Confession of sins led to the assignment of a penance, often taken from a list given in a Handbook for Confessors. In many cases, the severity of the penance might be alleviated by buying an indulgence. Indulgences were also sold to absolve people from the sin of not confessing to their own confessors. Mass was seen as a particularly effective form of intercession, and the practice of endowing masses to be said for the souls of those in purgatory meant that in larger churches masses would often be said at several altars at the same time, regardless of whether any congregation was present.

Technically outside the sacramental system, but imposed by the church and probably as important to people's daily lives as the sacraments, were other disciplines such as fasting, which included abstinence from meat on Fridays and from dairy products in Lent. Exemption from these rules could often be purchased for a fee. Many people's primary contact with the church was through the traditions of personal piety, including prayers and gifts to saints, and pilgrimages to holy places.

Luther's theology emerged out of a concern that these practices gave people the impression that they could earn salvation. He was worried that people thought of grace as something which needed to be – and indeed could be – earned through fasting or pilgrimage, or the buying of indulgences. It was very soon clear to him, however, that the sacraments, and particularly penance and the mass, had also become an essential aspect of what he condemned as an abusive system which tortured people's consciences and exploited their fears about salvation. "Any true Christian, whether living or dead, participates in all the blessings of Christ and the church; and this is granted him by God, even without indulgence letters," he asserted in the Ninety-Five Theses. It was clear that the "blessings of Christ and the church" must include the sacraments. Luther soon found himself pressed to say how many sacraments he thought there really were, and what he thought they meant.

In autumn 1519, Luther published three *Sermons* (so-called although they were probably never actually preached) on penance, baptism, and "the sacrament of the holy true body of Christ". These were written in German and dedicated to Margaret, Duchess of Brunswick and Luneburg, of whose "pious love of the Scriptures" Luther had received reports. He would not be writing about the remaining four sacraments, he commented in a letter to his friend George Spalatin, secretary to Frederick the Wise, "until I learn by what [scriptural] text I can prove that they are sacraments". A true sacrament was one which had been established by a divine promise of salvation. He did not believe this to be true of confirmation, unction, marriage or ordination. The following September, a further, and much more significant, work on the sacraments appeared. *On the Babylonian Captivity of the Church: A Prelude*, written in Latin, presented Luther's views on all seven late-medieval sacraments, arguing initially that the Eucharist, baptism and penance should properly be regarded as sacraments while the rest, although important, should not be regarded as sacraments. However, in the course of writing the treatise he became convinced that penance was not really a sacrament at all, and that only the Eucharist and baptism were true sacraments. A sacrament, Luther concluded, must be instituted by Christ using words which showed that it could mediate the promise of salvation. It must consist of a physical sign of the invisible grace it promised, and the sign must also be instituted by Christ. Penance, on this reading, was not a sacrament. Only baptism and the Eucharist were deserving of that title.

Although he would conclude in 1520 that it was not a sacrament, Luther was convinced that, properly understood, penance was of vital importance to all believers. He had argued in the Ninety-Five Theses that a believer's life should be one of repentance, and this, he believed, was made possible by confessing one's sins. Penance, he wrote in his 1519 *Sermon on Penance*, had three parts:

> The first is absolution. These are the words of the priest
> which show, tell, and proclaim to you that you are free and
> that your sins are forgiven you by God .... The second is
> grace, the forgiveness of sins, the peace and comfort of the
> conscience .... The third is faith, which firmly believes that
> the absolution and words of the priest are true, by the power
> of Christ's words, "Whatever you loose ... shall be loosed."

It was by virtue of the second part that Luther initially thought that penance should be called a sacrament. In 1519, he explained: "It is called a sacrament, a holy sign, because in it one hears the words externally that signify spiritual gifts within, gifts by which the heart is comforted and set at peace." A year later, in *Babylonian Captivity*, he reiterated the view that private confession was "useful, even necessary; ... a cure without equal for distressed consciences", for it made it possible to confess one's sins and to receive in faith the assurance that they had been forgiven. In *A Short Exhortation to Confession* (1529), he confirmed this view, but emphasized that private confession of sins should be the free choice of every individual. Luther did not think, however, that the confessor had to be a priest or that words of absolution had to be spoken by a priest. As he explained in 1519, assurance and comfort could be offered by a neighbour or any Christian: "Any Christian can say to you, 'God forgives you your sins ...' etc., and if you can accept that word with a confident faith, as though God were saying it to you, then in that same faith you are surely absolved." It was apparent that Luther's theology of the sacraments would have radical implications for his understanding of ordination and the role of the ordained priest or pastor.

Penance, in Luther's mature theological judgment, was not strictly a sacrament at all, although he valued it greatly. Baptism, on the other hand, most certainly was a sacrament. As he explained in *Babylonian Captivity*, Luther thought that baptism, in contrast to penance and the Eucharist, had not been "oppressed by the filthy and godless monsters of greed and superstition". The meaning of baptism, Luther thought, was that "the old man and the sinful birth of flesh and blood are to be wholly drowned by the grace of God" so that a spiritual birth takes place, through which the person baptized is "a child of grace and a justified person". Consequently, he believed that baptism should be done by full immersion, to symbolize not washing, but drowning and death: "The sinner does not so much need to be washed as he needs to die, in order to be wholly renewed and made another creature, and to be conformed to the death and resurrection of Christ, with whom he dies and rises again through baptism." Baptism therefore means renewal and regeneration. As he later put it in his lectures on Galatians: "In those who have been baptized a new light and flame arise; new and devout emotions come into being, such as fear and trust in God and hope; and a new will emerges." To be baptized is, as Paul says, to put on Christ. However, Luther noted in a sermon on baptism, "The significance of baptism – the dying or drowning of sin – is not fulfilled completely in this life." Baptism is an event, he thought, but it is also a process which continues throughout this mortal life: "The spiritual birth and the increase of grace and righteousness – even though it begins in baptism, lasts until death, indeed, until the Last Day." The life of the baptized is the life of the one who has been justified.

Although he did not believe that salvation is accomplished in baptism, Luther regarded baptism as important for salvation. In his 1519 *Sermon* he asserted that "baptism is an external sign or token, which so separates us from all men not baptized that we are thereby known as a people of Christ", suggesting that baptism might mark out the community of Christians. A year later, he was much more confident about this, writing that baptism must be understood as closely linked with salvation. The divine promise to which baptism points, Luther explained, could be found in Mark 16:16: "He who believes and is baptized will be saved." This was possible because God was the author of baptism, and the rite was a manifestation of God's promised salvation. Therefore, Luther asserted, we "must have no doubt whatever that, once we have been baptized, we are saved." The promise offered in baptism meant that baptism was all that is necessary for salvation; baptism, therefore, "must be set far above all the glitter of works, vows, religious orders, and whatever else man has introduced". In this reading, faith is the prerequisite for the efficacy of baptism – "unless faith is present or is conferred in baptism, baptism will profit us nothing". Consequently, in Luther's view "it is not baptism that justifies or benefits anyone, but it is faith in the word of promise to which baptism is added". Baptism, Luther seemed to be suggesting, marked out the true church which is the community of those who would be saved.

However, a few years later, Luther seemed to have changed his mind. In a treatise *On Temporal Authority: To What Extent it Should Be Obeyed* (1523), Luther emphasized that the act of baptism could never be enough, "for the world and the masses are and always will be un-Christian, even if they are all baptized and Christian in name". Baptism could not be effective without faith, he argued, but when it was effective it brought renewal and salvation. It was much more than a mark of church membership as Zwingli, for example, had suggested.

Given Luther's emphasis on the necessity of faith for effectual baptism, it was perhaps not surprising that some of his followers, among them Andreas Bodenstein von Karlstadt, interpreted his thinking on baptism as implying that children should not be baptized until they were old enough to profess their faith for themselves. Luther, however, remained a staunch advocate of infant baptism. In *Babylonian Captivity* he applied the example of the healing of the paralytic (Mark 2:3–12) "who was healed through the faith of others", to the situation of babies: "Infants are aided by the faith of others, namely, those who bring them for baptism. ... Through the prayer of the believing church which presents it, a prayer to which all things are possible [Mark 9:23], the infant is changed, cleansed, and renewed by inpoured faith."

Writing *Concerning Rebaptism* in 1528, he argued that no one but God can "discern the hearts of men and know whether or not they believe". Christ commanded that children be brought to him, and Scripture suggests that children "may and can believe, though they do not speak or understand". Luther concluded: "Faith does not exist for the sake of baptism, but baptism for the sake of faith. When faith comes, baptism is complete."

Luther's position on baptism changed little during his career, although his theology of baptism was honed by his defence of infant baptism and by his rejection of Zwingli's understanding of baptism as a human response to God's gift of grace, marking membership in the church. Despite their differences, which reflected fundamentally different beliefs about the nature of the sacraments, Zwingli, Luther and their followers were able to agree on a statement about baptism when they met at the Marburg Colloquy in 1529. The ninth of the Marburg Articles asserted

> that holy baptism is a sacrament which has been instituted by God as an aid to such a faith [i.e. to faith given by the Holy Spirit], and because God's command, "Go, baptize" [cf. Matthew 28:19], and God's promise, "He who believes" [Mark 16:16], are connected with it, it is therefore not merely an empty sign or watchword among Christians but, rather, a sign and work of God by which our faith grows and through which we are regenerated to eternal life.

The theology of baptism and the practice of believer's baptism would distinguish Anabaptists and other radical groups from those who came to be known as the "magisterial" reformers (those who worked with and through the magistrates and other political rulers), but it would not split mainstream Protestantism. The deepest rift in Protestantism would arise from differences over the theology of the Eucharist.

The Eucharist
Even in the midst of their heated discussions of the Eucharist, Luther and Zwingli found significant agreement in their rejection of traditional practice. The fifteenth article arising from the Marburg Colloquy listed several points of agreement:

We all believe and hold concerning the Supper of our dear
Lord Jesus Christ that both kinds should be used according
to the institution by Christ; also that the mass is not a work
with which one can secure grace for someone else, whether
he is dead or alive; also that the Sacrament of the Altar is a
sacrament of the true body and blood of Jesus Christ and
that the spiritual partaking of the same body and blood is
especially necessary for every Christian. Similarly, that the use
of the sacrament, like the word, has been given and ordained
by God Almighty in order that weak consciences may thereby
be excited to faith by the Holy Spirit.

The level of agreement was significant. Communion should
be given to the people in both kinds; that is, both as bread and
as wine. The mass could not benefit someone who was not
present. The sacrament strengthened – or even (for Luther)
gave rise to – faith. Partaking of the Eucharist was necessary
for every Christian, and at it Christians spiritually received
the body and blood of Christ. The theologians gathered at
Marburg disagreed on only one point, but it was crucial: "At
this time, we have not reached an agreement as to whether the
true body and blood of Christ are bodily present in the bread
and wine." Their different answers to the question of Christ's
presence in the Eucharistic elements divided Luther and his
followers from Zwingli and his. It would split the nascent
Reformation movement.

A decade earlier, in 1519, Luther had written his first
treatise on the Eucharist: *On the Sacrament of the Holy and
True Body of Christ*. In it he had called for the sacrament to
be offered in both kinds: that is, that the people be offered
both bread and wine, rather than receiving only the bread,

with just the priest partaking of the cup. The true meaning of the sacrament, he thought, was "fellowship of all the saints", echoed in the name "communion", derived from the Latin *communio*, "fellowship", which in turn derived from the Greek word *synaxis*. Through participation in this communion, he wrote, the believer could share in the "spiritual possessions of Christ and his saints", and Christ would make the burden of sin, sufferings and misfortune his own. Those who had received this benefit would respond by supporting their neighbour in their times of need and despair:

> Just as the bread is made out of many grains ground and mixed together, and out of the bodies of many grains there comes the body of one bread, in which each grain loses its form and body and takes upon itself the common body of the bread; and just as the drops of wine, in losing their own form, become the body of one common wine and drink – so it is and should be with us, if we use this sacrament properly. ... Through the interchange of [Christ's] blessings and our misfortunes, we become one loaf, one bread, one body, one drink, and have all things in common. ... In this way we are changed into one another and are made into a community by love. Without love there can be no such change.

Luther believed the community to be transformed by receiving the sacrament, in which, he said, the "natural flesh" of Christ is received:

> [Christ] gave his true natural flesh in the bread, and his natural true blood in the wine, that he might give a really perfect sacrament or sign. For just as the bread is changed

into his true natural body and the wine into his natural
true blood, so truly are we also drawn and changed into the
spiritual body.

This was made possible by the faith of the believer, through
which the communicant received, and was in turn transformed
by, Christ's body and blood.

At this stage in his career, Luther was insistent that the
transformation of the believer was what mattered:

It is more needful that you discern the spiritual than the natural
body of Christ; and faith in the spiritual body is more necessary
than faith in the natural body. For the natural without the
spiritual profits us nothing in this sacrament; a change must
occur [in the communicant] and be exercised through love.

The communal aspect of communion was important to
him, and he also emphasized that attending or receiving the
sacrament should not be seen as an automatic transfer of
grace. Believers must be directly involved, must believe, and
must be transformed.

Luther expounded his theological critique of the abuses of
the mass in *Babylonian Captivity* (1520). Here he identified
three "captivities" of the mass. First, he once more objected
to the fact that communion was offered in one kind. This,
he said, rendered the sacrament incomplete, and although he
cautioned, "I do not urge that both kinds be seized upon by
force," he hoped a General Council of the Church would put
an end to this abuse.

Secondly, Luther objected to the church's requirement of
belief in the doctrine of transubstantiation. Transubstantiation

taught that as the priest spoke Jesus' words in the prayer of consecration – "This is my body; this is my blood" – the substance (the very being, or essence) of the bread and wine were transformed into the substance (the very being, or essence) of Christ's body and blood, while their external appearance (colour, size, shape, taste; the so-called "accidents") remained unchanged. Luther's objection was that the doctrine of transubstantiation was based on the non-scriptural, Aristotelian terminology of substance and accidents. In 1520 he simply wanted to remove the stigma against those, like himself, who could not believe it. "What is asserted without the Scriptures or proven revelation may be held as an opinion, but need not be believed," he explained, so those who wanted to believe transubstantiation might, but should not insist that others must.

The third captivity, which he saw as "by far the most wicked abuse of all", was for Luther the fact that the mass had come to be regarded as "a good work and a sacrifice". In consequence, "the holy sacrament has been turned into mere merchandise, a market, and a profit-making business". The mass, he asserted, was God's gift to human beings, and not something that human beings offered to God.

Key to a proper understanding of the mass was, for Luther, the account of Christ's words at the Last Supper, which he drew from the Gospels of Matthew, Mark, and Luke, and from Paul in 1 Corinthians:

Now as they were eating, Jesus took bread, and blessed, and broke it, and gave it to his disciples and said, "Take, eat; this is my body, which is given for you." And he took a cup, and when he had given thanks he gave it to them, saying, "Drink of it, all of you; for this cup is the new testament in my blood, which is poured out for you and for many for the forgiveness of sins. Do this in remembrance of me."

For Luther, as he explained in *Babylonian Captivity*, Christ's use of the term "testament" showed the true meaning of the mass: "What we call the mass is a promise of the forgiveness of sins made to us by God, and such a promise as has been confirmed by the death of the Son of God." In the mass "life and salvation are freely promised, and actually granted to those who believe the promise". The faith of the believer makes it possible to "gather the fruits of the mass".

Luther took Christ's words "This is my body" to mean that Christ's physical body was really present in the bread and his blood in the wine. This understanding, he suggested in *Babylonian Captivity*, must be comprehended as a mystery to be grasped by faith. Just as faith can accept that Christ's human and divine natures "are simply there in their entirety" so that "it is truly said: 'This man is God; this God is man'", so too Christ's real body and the bread "both remain there at the same time, and it is truly said: 'This bread is my body; this wine is my blood,' and vice versa".

Luther never lost his conviction that Christ is really physically present in the bread and wine at the Eucharist. However, in the course of his controversy with Zwingli, he came to explain it in a different way. Christ's human body, he believed, took on the divine attribute of omnipresence – or, as Luther called it, ubiquity. In 1526, in a treatise directed against Karlstadt and his followers, entitled *The Sacrament of the Body and Blood of Christ – Against the Fanatics*, Luther asserted that Christ "is present everywhere, but he does not wish that you grope for him everywhere. Grope rather where the Word is, and there you will lay hold of him in the right way." Christ's presence in the Eucharist was a miracle, Luther suggested, like the miracle of the incarnation, or the miracle of growing crops, or the miracle that Christ could be received into the hearts of many hearers of the Word: "Christ does not permit himself to be divided into parts; yet he is distributed whole among all the faithful, so that one heart receives no less, and a thousand hearts no more, than the one Christ. This we must ever confess, and it is a daily miracle."

Christ had promised to be present to be received in the Eucharist. In Luther's opinion his body was indeed received. In believers it brought about eternal life, but in unbelievers it wrought their damnation.

Zwingli, however, rejected Luther's understanding of Christ's presence at the Eucharist. Although he believed that Christ's body and blood were received spiritually by believers as they remembered what Christ had done for them on the cross, he did not believe that Christ's human body could be objectively or physically present. The Eucharist was a means by which those who had already received the gift of God's forgiveness could express their thanks to God. Those who did not believe would receive only bread and wine. Christ's words "This is my body" should, Zwingli argued, be read metaphorically: "This *signifies* my body." Christ's human body was physically located in heaven, at the right hand of God, and therefore could not be present in the Eucharist. Luther disagreed with this. In a treatise directed against Zwingli and published in 1527, *That These Words "This is My Body" Still Stand Fast*, Luther explained: "The right hand of God is not a particular place where Christ's body is seated, as the fanatics dream, but is the power of God himself." He conceded that metaphorical language could sometimes be used in Scripture, but maintained that this was not such a case. Those who believed that Christ was physically present, he protested, "are not so foolish as to believe that Christ's body is in the bread in a crude visible manner, like bread in a basket or wine in a cup":

> The bright rays of the sun are so near you that they pierce into your eyes or your skin so that you feel it, yet you are unable to grasp them and put them into a box, even if you should try forever. Prevent them from shining in through the window – this you can do, but catch and grasp them you cannot. So too with Christ: although he is everywhere, he does not permit himself to be so caught and grasped.

Christ's objective, physical presence in the sacrament could not, for Luther, be doubted.

The heat of the disagreement with Zwingli did not blind Luther to the necessity of teaching what he saw as the "chief point" of the sacrament: the Word, by which he meant God's promise of forgiveness. The Lord's Supper, he wrote in the *Large Catechism*, is "bread and wine comprehended in, and connected with, the Word of God". It is received "that faith may refresh and strengthen itself … and become ever stronger and stronger". Soon after returning from Marburg in autumn 1529, Luther wrote an *Admonition Concerning the Sacrament of the Body and Blood of Our Lord*, in which he instructed pastors to encourage attendance at the Lord's Supper. In language which would have been much more acceptable to Zwingli and his followers he suggested that "the primary benefit and fruit which accrues to you from the use of the sacrament" is the reminder of the "favour and grace" given through Christ's death on the cross, and "the great, manifold, eternal need and death out of which he has rescued you".

Secondly, he argued, "Where such faith is thus continually refreshed and renewed, there the heart is also at the same time refreshed anew in its love of neighbour and is made strong and equipped to do all good works and to resist sin and all temptations of the devil." The language of community which had been so prominent in 1519 was not used here, but Luther confirmed his belief that the Eucharist would sustain the faithful and lead them to show their faith through works of love and charity.

Church and state

Luther's Reformation could not have taken place without the support of princes and city councils across the German lands. Although Luther initially formulated his critique of indulgences in terms which would have been quite familiar to his reform-minded contemporaries, the negative reaction of the papal authorities convinced him that he could look for no support from the church hierarchy. In 1520 he formulated an appeal *To the Christian Nobility of the German Nation*, dedicated to Charles V, in which he called on the emperor and the German princes and rulers to reform the church and purify it of abuses, if the church hierarchy would not.

In *To the Christian Nobility*, Luther identified three "walls" with which he claimed the "Romanists ... have protected themselves ... in such a way that no one has been able to reform them." The first, and for Luther the most significant, was the drawing of a distinction between spiritual and temporal, by which the church claimed to be beyond the jurisdiction of the temporal or secular authorities. In practice, the distinction between spiritual and temporal powers meant not only that clergy and members of religious orders were regarded as being spiritually superior to the laity, but also that they were subject to canon law rather than civic law. It was consequently difficult to prosecute clergy and members of religious orders who committed crimes. Moreover, church lands and the produce from them could not be taxed by civic authorities, which not infrequently made it possible for the produce of ecclesiastical lands to undercut local prices. Luther was most concerned about the claim to spiritual advantage, which he regarded as spurious and dangerously misleading. Many of his readers were probably angered by the financial and legal advantages, and attracted to his theology for its practical consequences.

To counteract the claims that clergy and those who had taken religious vows were spiritually superior, Luther argued that a priest or bishop was "nothing else but an officeholder". He pointed out that all those in authority, whether lay or ordained, "have been baptized with the same baptism, and have the same faith and the same gospel as the rest of us". Their authority was given to them by virtue of their office. Consequently "there is no true, fundamental difference between laymen and priests, princes and bishops, between religious and secular, except for the sake of office and work". Through baptism, everyone "can boast that he is already a consecrated priest, bishop, and pope" even though they may not have the office of preaching, but be "a cobbler, a smith, a peasant". Luther concluded:

> Those who are now called "spiritual", that is, priests, bishops, or popes, are neither different from other Christians nor

superior to them, except that they are charged with the administration of the word of God and the sacraments, which is their work and office.

The office was what gave them their authority, but it did not give them some special status with God. Similarly, the temporal authorities "[bore] the sword and rod in their hand to punish the wicked and protect the good". Everyone should fall under the jurisdiction of these authorities, "regardless of whether it is pope, bishop, or priest whom it affects. Whoever is guilty, let him suffer."

Through this doctrine, which came to be known as the priesthood of all believers, Luther emphasized that it was baptism, and not ordination or vows, which mattered in defining the Christian. This did not imply that he believed that everyone who had been baptized was actually called by God to preach the Word or to celebrate the sacraments. Those tasks, he thought, needed special authorization, although this need not necessarily be episcopal ordination:

> Suppose a group of earnest Christian laymen were taken prisoner and set down in a desert without an episcopally ordained priest among them. And suppose they were to come to a common mind there and then in the desert and elect one of their number, whether he were married or not, and charge him to baptize, say mass, pronounce absolution, and preach the gospel. Such a man would be as truly a priest as though he had been ordained by all the bishops and popes in the world.

In cases of necessity, he argued, baptism and absolution could be offered by any baptized Christian. Moreover, every

Christian has a responsibility to ensure that the Word of God is preached. Consequently, if the ecclesiastical authorities would not appoint a preacher, then the congregation could do so. In 1523, in support of the town of Leising, which had introduced the Reformation and appointed a pastor against the will of the local abbot, who had the right of appointment, Luther wrote a treatise defending this position: *That a Christian Assembly or Congregation Has the Right and Power to Judge All Teaching and to Call, Appoint, and Dismiss Teachers, Established and Proven by Scripture.* Just a few years later, however, Luther would revise this view, when his conviction that all people were equal before God on account of their baptism, coupled with the idea that a congregation might appoint its own preacher, proved to have consequences that he had neither foreseen nor welcomed.

In 1520, Luther seemed to be arguing that the church might properly be subject to temporal authorities. However, it was not long before he found himself in opposition to those authorities. The following year, Luther was summoned before the emperor, Charles V, at the Diet of Worms, and instructed to recant. He did not. The emperor responded with the Edict of Worms, which condemned Luther to an existence as a stateless person, and forbade the sale of his books in the German territories. In a number of these territories, Luther's works were suppressed or burned. Although some rulers did introduce church reforms inspired by Luther's theology into their territories, Luther came to the conclusion that many princes could not be trusted to reform the church. In his treatise *On Temporal Authority: To What Extent it Should Be Obeyed*, written in 1523, he presented a new understanding of the relationship between the spiritual and the temporal. While he affirmed that both were established and ordained by God, he had now come to see them as distinct, with important but different functions and responsibilities. He wrote: "Both must be permitted to remain; the one to produce righteousness, the other to bring about external peace and prevent evil deeds." Although he believed that those who truly live in Christ have no need of temporal government, Luther now concluded that they were a minority. Temporal government, he had come to believe, was for the majority a necessary restraint.

Luther argued that since it had been instituted by God, temporal government must be obeyed, whether it was just – as God intended – or not. The Gospel required Christians to bear the injustice they suffer. However, it also commanded them to resist injustice meted out to others. Therefore, he exhorted, "In what concerns you and yours, you govern yourself by the gospel and suffer injustice toward yourself as a true Christian; in what concerns the person or property of others, you govern yourself according to love and tolerate no injustice toward your neighbour." Unjust rulers could and should be resisted on behalf of others. Similarly, Christians could – and in certain circumstances should – "serve God in government". Luther did not advocate that Christians should withdraw from the responsibilities of temporal rule.

In matters of the Gospel, however, he thought that temporal powers should not attempt to control people's consciences. In questions such as the banning of the German New Testament by secular authorities, Luther recommended a policy of what might now be called passive or non-violent resistance:

In Meissen, Bavaria, the Mark Brandenburg, and other places, the tyrants have issued an order that all copies of the New Testament are everywhere to be turned in to the officials. This should be the response of their subjects: They should not turn in a single page, not even a letter, on pain of losing their salvation. Whoever does so is delivering Christ up into the hands of Herod, for these tyrants act as murderers of Christ just like Herod. If their homes are ordered [to be] searched and books or property taken by force, they should suffer it to be done. Outrage is not to be resisted but endured; yet we should not sanction it, or lift a little finger to conform, or obey.

Temporal power should not seek to exercise power over faith or conscience; its sphere should remain the physical aspects of life, such as behaviour and property. Christian princes, whom Luther by now believed to be few and far between, should be wholeheartedly concerned for "the benefit, honour, and salvation of others", directing their actions towards ensuring the well-being of their subjects, and not seeking merely to serve their own ends. Such a prince, thought Luther, would pray for wisdom to rule well and deal justly with evil-doers. He would be a good Christian with a calling to be a good prince. Luther would later concede that if no candidates could be found who were qualified to lead the church, then such a Christian prince might act as an emergency bishop, or *Notbischof*. In 1523, he suggested that even apparently evil rulers might also be doing the will of God. They should be seen as "God's executioners and hangmen; his divine wrath uses them to punish the wicked and to maintain outward peace." God might use whatever tools he chose, including ungodly rulers.

Luther's strong sense that temporal government represented divinely instituted order was strengthened by his experiences of the uprisings and civic unrest of the mid-1520s. The protests that gave rise to the farmers' uprisings were often led by bailiffs, mayors or other local political figures, members of guilds, yeomen farmers, or even reformers. The leaders, at least, were often educated, and from the early 1520s onwards, many had read Luther's works and were attracted by his language of freedom. As violence threatened to erupt in 1525, Luther wrote an *Admonition to Peace* in response to the Twelve Articles of Swabia, which formulated some of the demands of the farmers and peasants. In it, Luther pointed the finger of blame at the princes and lords, both secular and ecclesiastical, who, he said, had failed to accept his preaching of the Gospel and had in addition exploited the people:

> You do not cease to rant and rave against the holy gospel, even though you know that it is true and that you cannot refute it. In addition, as temporal rulers you do nothing but cheat and rob the people so that you may lead a life of luxury and extravagance. The poor common people cannot bear it any longer.

Luther urged the princes to accept the Gospel, seek reconciliation with those who threatened to attack them, moderate their demands upon the farmers and peasants, and reform their ways of living. Luther acknowledged that many of the demands set forth in the Twelve Articles were just. However, he told the peasants that what they were doing was worse than the injustices perpetrated by their lords, for they were going against God's law: "The rulers unjustly take your property; that is the one side. On the other hand, you take from them their authority, in which their whole property and life and being consist." This, Luther argued, was against the natural law which was shared by all people, whether Christian or not. Christians, however, had even more reason not to offer violent resistance to injustice: "Christ says that we should not resist evil or injustice but always yield, suffer, and let things be taken from us." Consequently, Luther maintained that the farmers and peasants were wrong to use force in an attempt to achieve justice. They were also wrong to claim that the Gospel justified or sanctioned such actions. Christian law, he thought, required submission to divinely instituted authority, and not violence and insurrection.

Luther made this point even more strongly in his later treatise, *Against the Robbing and Murdering Hordes of Peasants*. Here he accused the farmers and peasants of having committed "three terrible sins against God and man". For this reason "they have abundantly merited death in body and soul". They had broken their oaths of fealty to their rulers; they had robbed, plundered, and murdered; and they had claimed Christ's authority for their crimes. The first two were temporal crimes; the third was, in Luther's eyes, blasphemy. With very unfortunate timing, Luther's treatise was published only after a massacre in which thousands of the insurgents were killed.

Luther continued to maintain that, as Paul put it in Galatians 2:6: "God shows no partiality". As he had said in 1520, in matters of faith all were equal in the eyes of God through their baptism. However, that in no way countered or relativized the need for hierarchical order in society:

> In this world God wants the observance of order, respect, and
> a distinction among social positions. Otherwise the child or
> the pupil or the subject or the servant would say: "I am just as
> much a Christian as my father or teacher or prince or master!

So why should I respect him?" Therefore God wants the difference of social position to be observed among us – not in the sight of God, where the distinction ceases.

That is, as he had written to Erasmus, "Where religion and the Word of God are the issue, there must be no partiality; but apart from religion, apart from God, there must be respect of persons and partiality; for otherwise confusion would result." Equality and freedom in the eyes of God did not mean equality and freedom in secular society.

From Luther to Lutheranism

Luther's theology was worked out amid conflict and crisis. It showed his interest in educating the common people in the faith, and his wish to convince his theologically trained colleagues that his theological insights proclaimed Gospel truth. It was shaped by the immediacy of his concerns, by his marked and often polemical views, by his excoriating attacks on his opponents. It was formed by his need to balance his vision of personal faith against his desire for orderly society in which the Gospel could be truly preached. All of this made it very difficult even for his contemporaries to identify what Luther had really said. Luther had criticized the papacy for seeking to control interpretation of Scripture. In his turn he had sought to define the true interpretation of the Gospel, and his followers were faced with the task of understanding what he had meant.

Luther died on 18 February 1546. Almost immediately the fragile balance of power between Electoral Saxony and Ducal Saxony tipped into open warfare. Duke Moritz of Saxony, supported by Emperor Charles V, gained the upper hand. Then Duke Moritz captured his cousin, Elector John Frederick of Saxony, together with Philip of Hesse (also Moritz's father-in-law), and in the subsequent negotiations, Moritz assumed the electoral title and John Frederick was forced to cede to him substantial territories, including Wittenberg. In 1548 Charles V imposed the Augsburg "Interim", intended as a temporary measure until the Council of Trent, called by Pope Paul III, which had held its first group of sessions between 1545 and 1548, could bring about a religious settlement. The Interim outlawed all Protestant practices except clerical marriage and communion in both kinds. Resistance to it demonstrated just how successfully the Reformation had established itself in some areas. It was not long before the Interim proved unenforceable, and war once more broke out. In 1555 the Peace of Augsburg established the principle of *cuius regio eius religio* (the religion of the one who rules) in the German Empire: the people's faith should be defined by the faith of the ruler. Provided that the ruler was not a bishop, he might dictate whether religion in his territory should be defined by appeal either to the Augsburg Confession or to the pope. Imperial cities must make provision for both forms of religion. The faith of Luther as stated in the Augsburg Confession had achieved legal status in the empire.

But what was that faith? The period from 1549 until 1556 was characterized by a series of controversies over the proper interpretation of Luther's teachings and over the place of Philip Melanchthon's works. The theologians argued about which parts of the liturgy could be considered "matters of indifference" or *adiaphora* – about the proper understanding of justification; about the role of good works in salvation; about the Eucharist; over the question of whether human beings can cooperate in salvation; and about whether the law had a specific use for those who were justified. It would be another twenty years before a further definitive statement of faith was drafted: the Formula of Concord (1577), which attempted to resolve the differences. Many of these controversies reflected the growing influence of the most significant figure of the second generation of reformers: John Calvin.

PART II

JOHN CALVIN

CHAPTER 3

CALVIN'S CONTEXT

Child of the church

Jean Cauvin – as his name was spelt in French – was born in 1509 in Noyon, in northern France, making him a whole generation younger than Martin Luther. His father, Girard Cauvin, had risen from an artisan background to become the secretary to the Bishop of Noyon, and subsequently lawyer to the cathedral chapter. His mother, Jeanne Le Franc, was the daughter of an innkeeper and merchant in Cambrai. She bore three further sons and died when Calvin was just six years old. His father remarried and Calvin had two half-sisters from his father's second marriage.

As a boy, Calvin was destined for an ecclesiastical career, and from the age of twelve, he received financial support from the church for his education. Initially Calvin was granted a quarter of the income from the altar of La Gésine in Noyon Cathedral. In 1527 he was also awarded the curate's income from the parish of

St Martin de Martheville, some twenty-five miles from Noyon. Two years later, this income was replaced by that from Pont-l'Evêque, a village just outside Noyon where his father's family had been boatmen. He drew this income until 1534. Calvin was not expected to offer his services directly to either of these parishes. Medieval absenteeism paid for his education.

With the help of this ecclesiastical income, Calvin began his formal education in Noyon, where he was taught with the bishop's nephews. At fourteen he was sent to Paris to continue his studies at the Collège de La Marche. He was taught by one of the foremost French Latinists of the time, Mathurin Cordier, whom Calvin later invited to be principal of the school in Geneva. Soon afterwards, he moved to the Collège Montaigu, a centre of traditionalist theology and opposition to Luther's ideas. Luther's writings had been condemned by the Sorbonne in 1521, but many of his treatises were quite readily available in French translation. Calvin may here have been introduced to Luther's ideas through criticism of them. He would remain opposed to evangelical theology until his early twenties. Erasmus and the satirical author François Rabelais had both studied at the Collège Montaigu and were uncomplimentary about its scholastic emphasis. Calvin, however, never criticized his education there, and it was probably the Collège Montaigu which introduced him not only to scholastic theology – and perhaps particularly nominalism, as taught by John Mair, or Major – but also to the Church Fathers, including Augustine.

Calvin had been destined for the priesthood, but in 1527 his father decided that his son should instead study law. It is likely that by this time Calvin's father was already embroiled in a dispute with the ecclesiastical authorities in Noyon which would see him excommunicated – a state of affairs which, upon his death in 1535, would make it difficult for him to be buried in consecrated ground. Obedient to his father's wishes, Calvin left Paris to continue his studies in Orléans and Bourges. Here the emphasis was not on canon law, as would have been the case in Paris, but on civil law. Calvin was introduced to the use of humanist approaches which regarded jurisprudence as an aspect of moral philosophy and explored the ethical implications of legal texts, as well as their context and the ideas and principles which shaped them. The approach to legal texts which Calvin learnt in Orléans would later be of fundamental importance in shaping his approach to Scripture.

Calvin took to his legal studies with enthusiasm. He was a brilliant student, one of the best of his year, and soon gained a reputation as a humanist scholar. Theodore Beza later recorded that Calvin regularly worked from early in the morning until after midnight. His later health problems have been associated with this rigorous regime. Alongside his legal studies, he learnt Greek from the humanist philologist and jurist Melchior Volmar, to whom he would later dedicate his commentary on Paul's second letter to the Corinthians. Volmar had strong reforming interests, but it is not clear how significant an influence he had on Calvin. Certainly Calvin seemed at this stage to retain his allegiance to the Roman church, but he was building up a network of humanist-inclined friends and teachers who would remain important to him once he himself became a supporter of the evangelical cause.

Humanism and reform in France
Calvin's encounter with humanism emerged in the context of growing interest in humanist approaches in France during

the early decades of the sixteenth century. These interests were furthered by the king, François I, who came to the throne in 1515 having received an education which encouraged his interest in the art and architecture of the Italian Renaissance and exposed him to humanist ideas. François supported leading artists such as Leonardo da Vinci, Michelangelo, Titian, and Raphael. He furthered the careers of leading French humanists such as Guillaume Budé, whom he appointed as his librarian and who encouraged him to invest in humanist education. François established the Collège Royal and endowed several lectureships, the *Lecteurs Royaux*.

François's interest in humanist and Renaissance ideas was balanced, and to some extent mitigated, by his dynastic interests. In 1515, after a decisive victory over Swiss and papal troops at Marignano, he had quickly moved to define the relationship between France and the papacy. The resulting Concordat of Bologna was signed in 1516. It confirmed the right of the king of France to tithe clergy and to restrict their right of appeal to Rome, and also his power to appoint archbishops, bishops, abbots and priors. In return, the pope was authorized to collect from French benefices all the revenue that accrued during the first year after a new appointment, and François conceded that the pope's powers were not subject to a council (in part a response to attempts by his predecessor, Louis XII, to convoke a council at Pisa in 1511). The Concordat superseded an earlier agreement between the pope and the French king, the "Pragmatic Sanction" of 1438, which had given the king of France powers to tax the clergy, to try clergy and members of religious orders in lay courts, and to appoint bishops and abbots. Through the Concordat, the papacy ceded to the French king many of the powers which rulers elsewhere gained through introducing the Reformation.

The king's sister, Marguerite d'Angoulême – Queen of Navarre after her marriage to Henri d'Albret in 1527 – was also well known for her humanist interests. To a greater extent than her brother, Marguerite was a supporter of humanist church reform, and she furthered the interests of a circle of reforming humanists, including the biblical scholar Jacques Lefèvre and the abbot, later bishop, Guillaume Briçonnet, whom in 1521 she invited to become her spiritual director.

As Abbot of St-Germain-des-Près from 1507, Briçonnet introduced reforms to religious life and encouraged humanist scholarship. He was much influenced by the work of Lefèvre, to whom he had been introduced by Lefèvre's colleague Josse van Clichtove, Bishop of Tournai from 1519 and of Chartres from 1521, who was himself a humanist but would become a strong opponent of Lutheran reform. Briçonnet invited Lefèvre to live in the abbey, where Lefèvre prepared his *Quincuplex Psalterium*, an edition of the Psalms in French, Latin, Hebrew and Greek with his own translation and comments (1509), and a commentary on Paul's epistles (1512) which would later be used by Luther in preparing his Romans lectures. Briçonnet was appointed Bishop of Meaux, near Paris, in 1516. His diocese became the centre for a loose association of evangelical humanists, often called the "Circle of Meaux", who shared an interest in the study of Scripture and sought to return to the faith and practice of the early church.

Those who gathered in Meaux were inspired by humanist approaches to texts, but they went on to take very different attitudes towards reform. They included Lefèvre; his student Gérard Roussel, who in 1525 fled with Lefèvre to Strasbourg and subsequently returned to France under the protection of Marguerite de Navarre, becoming Abbot of Clairac in 1527 and Bishop of Oléron in 1536; Guillaume Farel, later the reformer of Geneva and other parts of French-speaking Switzerland, and an important influence on Calvin; Pierre Caroli, who would later be appointed evangelical preacher in Lausanne, a position from which he would accuse Farel and Calvin of heresy; Martial Mazurier, who was banned from preaching in 1525 but later seems to have become a lecturer at the Sorbonne, where he took an early interest in the *Exercises* of Ignatius of Loyola; and the Hebraist François Vatable.

Briçonnet was active in preaching and visiting the congregations of his diocese, enquiring as to whether the clergy were preaching the Gospel, but he was also concerned to preserve orthodoxy, particularly after the condemnation of Luther's writings by the Sorbonne in 1521. In April 1523, he took steps to prevent the preaching of Luther's theology in his diocese, whereupon Farel and others left Meaux in protest. In 1525, while François was being held in captivity by the emperor Charles V, Briçonnet was investigated by the theologians of the Sorbonne. The Circle of Meaux was dispersed, and many of its members fled to Strasbourg, although Briçonnet continued to lead the diocese until shortly before his death in 1534.

Calvin encountered humanist ideas in the midst of these controversies. By the time he returned to Paris in 1531 or 1532, the situation of those interested in biblical humanism and evangelical reform had become precarious. This was the point at which Calvin himself underwent what he in the introduction to his *Commentary on Psalms* would describe as his "sudden" or "unexpected" conversion which, he said, "subdued and brought my mind to a teachable frame". He was, he wrote, "too obstinately devoted to the superstitions of Popery to be easily extricated from so profound an abyss of mire"; his mind was "more hardened in such matters than might have been expected from one at my early period of life". During this period he prepared his first scholarly work for publication. This was a commentary on Seneca's *De clementia*, a humanist endeavour which appeared in 1532 and showed no obvious interest in theological matters. However, he wrote later, "Before a year had elapsed, those who had any desire for purer doctrine were continually coming to me to learn, although I myself was as yet but a mere novice and beginner." By the winter of 1533–34, Calvin had become a known supporter of evangelical reform.

During 1533, a number of events brought the situation of the Reform party in France to a head. The authorities were alarmed when, in the spring, Gérard Roussel, formerly a preacher in Meaux, gave a series of Lent sermons which attracted congregations of thousands. Then, on 1 November, the incoming rector of the University of Paris, Nicolas Cop, gave his inaugural lecture, which took the form of a sermon. Cop took as his text the lectionary reading for All Saints' Day, the Beatitudes (Matthew 5:3–11), which he expounded with the help of a Christian Erasmian philosophy complemented by a juxtaposition of Law and Gospel reminiscent of Luther's theology:

The Law mentions the mercy of God, but only on a definite condition: provided the Law be fulfilled. The Gospel freely offers forgiveness of sins and justification. We have in fact not been accepted by God because we fulfil the Law's demands, but only because of the promise of Christ; if a man doubts this promise, he cannot live a godly life and is preparing himself for the fires of hell.

François was outraged, and wrote to his *parlement* deploring what had happened: "We are very troubled and displeased at what has taken place in our beloved city of Paris, chief and capital of our kingdom, and where at the principal university of Christendom that accursed heretical Lutheran sect swarms." He instructed measures to be taken against Cop and his followers. Cop fled to Basel, and Calvin, who had almost certainly either helped Cop to compose his address or written it himself, although he remained in Paris, took the assumed name Charles d'Espeville.

A reformer in exile
By spring 1534, Calvin was explicitly identifying himself with reforming teachings, and rejected the authority of the papal church. In May he went to Noyon and renounced his ecclesiastical income. Benefiting from the resumption of an attitude of relative tolerance towards the reform-minded on François's part, Calvin then spent several months travelling through France, visiting Navarre where he met Lefèvre at the court of Marguerite de Navarre. Calvin wrote his first theological treatise at this time, *On the Sleep of the Soul*, which argued against the idea that the soul slept until the resurrection. He probably also began to draft the catechetical work which would become his *Institutes of Christian Religion*.

The *affair des placards* – affair of the placards – in October brought this phase to an end. Antoine Marcourt, a French evangelical who had gone into exile in Neuchâtel, had posters and flysheets printed which criticized the mass. On the night of 17–18 October these were posted in and around Paris (even, it was said, on the king's bedroom door). François and his advisors reacted immediately to what they saw as an attack on the state, ordering arrests and executions. Realizing that he was now *persona non grata* with the French authorities, Calvin, together with his friend, the biblical humanist Louis du Tillet, left France for Strasbourg and Basel.

After a brief stay in Strasbourg, Calvin and du Tillet arrived in Basel in January 1536. The city was an important centre of the humanist printing industry, and Erasmus had been based there since 1516. The city council had introduced the Reformation in 1529, assisted by Johannes Oecolampadius, who had originally been invited to become the city's preacher by Basel's bishop, Christoph von Utenheim, in order to further von Utenheim's vision of church reform. By 1529, von Utenheim had moved the episcopal residence out of the city. When the city council decided to introduce the Reformation, the cathedral chapter, and with them Erasmus, left for Freiburg-im-Breisgau. Erasmus returned to Basel in 1535, only to die of typhus in July of the following year.

In Basel, Calvin met influential humanist reformers such as Simon Grynaeus and Oswald Myconius, recently returned from introducing the Reformation into south-German Württemberg, and Heinrich Bullinger, Zwingli's successor in Zürich. He probably read some or all of Zwingli's Latin works – Calvin's German was never good – and studied Hebrew.

He wrote two prefaces to the translation of the Bible into French by his cousin Pierre-Robert Olivetan, the first edition of which had been published in Neuchâtel in 1535, as well as completing the first edition of the *Institutes*, which was printed in Basel in 1536.

The first edition of the *Institutes* had a double function. Modelled on Luther's catechisms, it explored the Law by means of the Ten Commandments, faith by means of the Apostles' Creed, and prayer by means of the Lord's Prayer; continued with a discussion of the true and false sacraments; and concluded with a discussion of Christian freedom, ecclesiastical power, and civil power. The work was dedicated to François I, to whom Calvin addressed a substantial introductory epistle. In it he explained his reasons for writing. Most importantly, he wanted to offer a means of experiencing Christ and understanding what it meant to lead a godly life:

> My purpose was solely to transmit certain rudiments by
> which those who are touched with any zeal for religion might
> be shaped to true godliness. And I undertook this labour
> especially for our French countrymen, very many of whom
> I saw to be hungering and thirsting for Christ; very few of
> whom had been imbued with even a slight knowledge of him.

To this extent, the *Institutes* grew out of Calvin's own faith, and his experience of teaching and preaching the Gospel. Additionally, however, as he remembered it in 1557, Calvin wished to clear the name of those of good conscience who had been accused of being Anabaptists or radicals, and to show that French claims that all those executed were Anabaptists were simply not true.

As Calvin worked on the *Institutes*, the German city of Münster had become subject to the radical rule of a group of Anabaptists. Anabaptist rule in Münster had begun with the city council's decision in 1532 to invite Bernd Rothmann, an evangelical preacher, to proclaim the Reformation in the city – a procedure which was no different from the introduction of the Reformation in most other German cities. Rothmann, however, proved increasingly attracted by Anabaptist teachings. His supporters took control of the city, expelling the city council and many citizens, and replacing them with radicals who came to Münster from across Germany and the Netherlands. Their self-proclaimed leaders, Jan Matthijs and Jan van Leiden, announced the second coming of Christ at Easter 1534. They declared the city to be the new Jerusalem, removing rights of private ownership, destroying the city's records, requisitioning the best houses, and entering into polygamous marriage. From just before Easter 1534, Franz von Waldeck, the prince-bishop of Münster, besieged the city, which finally fell in June of the following year. The shocking story of Münster was a gift to the opponents of Luther's reforms, who claimed that it revealed the true colours of all reformers.

In France, the executions of those involved in the *affaire des placards* had been justified on the grounds that only "Anabaptists and seditious persons" had been persecuted, and that they "by their perverse ravings and false opinions, were overthrowing not only religion but also all civil order". Calvin intended the *Institutes* to show that this was not the case. Protestants, he assured the French king, could be as law-abiding as the followers of the old faith. And French Protestants, he assured the world outside France – a world where his Latin work could be read at least as easily as it could be in France – were being persecuted and executed for preaching the Gospel, and not for holding radical or Anabaptist views.

Having seen the *Institutes* to the press, Calvin and du Tillet set off for Lombardy, in northern Italy. Calvin had been invited to the court of Renée de France, daughter of Louis XII and sister-in-law of François I, who was strongly committed to reform. There he also made the acquaintance of the French poet Clément Marot, who had fled Paris for Ferrara in 1534. In 1542, Marot would become a refugee in Geneva. His translations of the Psalms were a significant popularizing factor in the French Reformed tradition. The meeting with Renée de France was an important one for both of them. Calvin became Renée's chief spiritual advisor and retained this role for the rest of his life. His final letter in 1564 would be addressed to her.

From Ferrara, Calvin wrote a number of surviving letters, two of which show how he was beginning to take on the role of spiritual advisor, not only to queens, but to his own circle of acquaintances. He advised his friend Nicolas Duchemin to avoid attendance at the mass, any kind of honouring of images, the acquisition of indulgences, and any involvement in the giving of extreme unction. The practicalities and difficulties of the life of a Gospel believer in a Catholic milieu were very clear to him. Calvin also wrote to Gérard Roussel, recently nominated by Marguerite de Navarre as Bishop of Oloron, emphasizing in terms reminiscent of Luther's the responsibility of ordained ministers to preach the Word. He warned Roussel that he must bear the responsibility for the souls of all those led astray by the practices of the Roman church in which he would serve. In Calvin's opinion, there could be only one response: to resign the office of bishop. In a few short years, Calvin had entirely abandoned his own church upbringing.

In May 1536, Calvin and du Tillet returned to Basel. Hearing that the persecution in France was lessening, Calvin decided to continue to France, where he wished to set his affairs in order. He also spent time with his brother and sister, Antoine and Marie, whom he persuaded to emigrate with him to Strasbourg, where they could begin a new life of freedom of belief in the French exile community. The direct route to Strasbourg was closed as a result of the movement of troops in preparation for a further bout of hostilities between François I and Charles V. Calvin and his party decided to travel instead via Geneva, where the Reformation had been introduced that spring with the assistance of Guillaume Farel. They arrived there, intending to spend just one night, on 8 August 1536. It was to prove a fateful detour.

Scholar turned preacher – Calvin's first Genevan period (1536–38)

Looking back at his arrival in Geneva from the vantage point of the end of his career, Calvin remembered its circumstances:

> Since the most direct road to Strasbourg, where I intended to settle, was closed by the war, I had intended to travel quickly via Geneva without spending more than a single night in that city. Not long before this, popery had been driven from it by the exertions of the excellent person whom I named above [i.e. Guillaume Farel] and Peter [i.e. Pierre] Viret. However, the situation was still unsettled, and the city was divided into vicious and dangerous factions. A person who has now disgracefully apostatised and returned to the Papists [i.e. du Tillet, who in 1538 would renounce his Protestant beliefs] made known my presence [in Geneva] to others.

Farel, burning with an extraordinary zeal to advance the gospel, sought with all his powers to make me stay. When he learned that my heart was set on devoting myself to private studies, and could not persuade me to stay, he swore that God would curse the tranquillity of my studies if I went on and did not stay to help him, when the need was so urgent. I was so stricken with terror that I gave up any idea of continuing my journey. However, sensible of my natural bashfulness and shyness, I would not promise to discharge any particular office.

Giving in to Farel's importuning, Calvin decided to remain in Geneva. Apart from a brief period in exile in Strasbourg, the city would become the theatre of his ministry for the rest of his life.

In the early sixteenth century, Geneva was technically part of the Duchy of Savoy, to which the more rural Genévois area had been annexed in 1415. However, it was effectively an independent city, ruled by a prince-bishop who was – as his predecessors had been throughout the fifteenth century – a member of the family of the Counts of Savoy. Pierre de la Baume had been made Bishop of Geneva in 1522. He had fled Geneva in 1533 and returned, only to be expelled from the city in 1535 as a result of the Reformation. However, the bishop's authority had been subject to challenge by the city's own structures of government for some time. The Genevan council had claimed the right of self-rule which had been granted to the city in 1387, and in 1527 the bishop had ceded the administration of justice to the city's citizens.

Authority within the city was exercised by a hierarchy of councils. The citizens of Geneva, whether native-born citoyens or naturalized bourgeois, made up the *Conseil Générale*, which met annually to ratify laws and elect magistrates. From among their number was chosen the Council of Two Hundred (the Large Council), which was made up of representatives from each of the city's neighbourhoods. From the Large Council were chosen a Council of Sixty and a Small Council of about twenty members, presided over by four civil magistrates or syndics, which dealt with foreign affairs and made most of the important decisions relating to the running of the city. The Large Council voted on measures presented by the Small Council, set wine and grain prices, and elected judges. The interests of the city's householders thus directly shaped the governance of the city.

The citizens' interests also shaped the city's politics. Geneva's geographic location meant that the city was engaged in three key sets of relationships. To the south lay Savoy, to which the city had technically belonged for the past century. The bishop and his supporters looked to Savoy for support and identity. To the north and west lay France, important in terms of trade. To the east lay the Pays du Vaud, which in the 1520s and 1530s was being drawn into membership of the Swiss Confederation through the efforts of (or, perhaps better, annexation by) the city of Bern. For the Swiss, extending the Confederation still further to include Geneva offered the possibility of improved access to the important trade routes between France and Italy. For many in Geneva, membership of the Confederation appeared to offer a guarantee of Genevan independence and self-determination, and the rejection of the influence of the Savoyard in the person of the prince-bishop. Similarly, the introduction of the Reformation promised freedom from the ecclesiastical, and self-determination in questions of religion.

The Reformation had been introduced into Geneva under the direction of Guillaume Farel. Having fled Meaux in

1521, Farel had gone first to Basel, where he was taken in by Basel's reformer, Johannes Oecolampadius, and initially given permission to teach theology and to preach. Soon, however, he was silenced and expelled, possibly on Erasmus's initiative. Farel moved on to Strasbourg, where he encountered Martin Bucer and Wolfgang Capito. In 1524, he was invited by the young Duke Ulrich of Württemberg to help introduce the Reformation into Monbéliard (called in German Mompelgard), the duke's French-speaking territory. Returning the next year to Strasbourg and then to Basel, he was appointed preacher in Aigle, a village near Lausanne. From there he became involved with the introduction of the Reformation in Bern, Neuchâtel and the Pays de Vaud. In 1529, Farel wrote the *Summaire*, the first presentation of the evangelical faith in French, and he also drafted the first French liturgies for the Lord's Supper and baptism, the *Manière et fasson*. Farel began preaching in Geneva in 1532. He initially encountered strong opposition, which forced him to leave. However, with the support of the Bern city council, he returned to Geneva the following March. In January 1534 he organized a theological disputation, despite the opposition of the bishop, and in March, after repeated requests from the Bernese, he received permission to preach in the Franciscan church.

In June 1535, Farel staged a formal theological disputation with Pierre Caroli, another former member of the Meaux circle and prominent French refugee. Caroli would later become an outspoken opponent of Farel and Calvin, but for now he supported Farel's efforts. That August, Farel called for the destruction of images in Geneva's churches. The statues and stained windows were removed from the Cathedral of St Pierre, and its walls were partially whitewashed. The suppression of the mass followed, by order of the Small Council, at which point the cathedral chapter and many other clergy and religious left the city. By January 1536, a form of evangelical order had been introduced in Geneva. Most festivals and holidays other than Sundays were suppressed, fonts were removed from the churches, and mass was replaced by the Lord's Supper, celebrated in French using ordinary leavened bread rather than unleavened hosts. On 21 May 1536, the *Conseil Générale* formally expressed its assent to the introduction of the Reformation.

Calvin began his ministry in Geneva with a series of lectures on the Greek text of Paul's epistles – probably focusing on Romans – which he offered to a group that gathered in the cathedral. He also taught the New Testament to the students of Geneva's Latin school. When Farel argued that Calvin should be paid for this work, the council clerk did not even know Calvin's name, describing him simply as *ille Gallus* – "that Frenchman". In October Calvin took part in a disputation in Lausanne in support of the Reformation of the Pays de Vaud, allying himself with Caroli, Farel, and Pierre Viret, another French exile who became preacher in Lausanne, facing immense difficulties as the Bernese minority sought to impose the reformed faith on an unwilling Catholic majority. Realizing the need for the Reformation in Geneva to be based on sound teaching, both understood and accepted by the people, Calvin and Farel worked on a combined catechism and confession of faith together with a church order – the *Instruction et confession de foy dont on use en l'église de Genève* and *Articles concernant l'organisation de l'église et du culte* – intended to inform and regulate religious life in Geneva. The *Articles* required all citizens to take an oath affirming the confession of faith, mandated the use of the catechism as a basis for instructing children, introduced a weekly celebration of the Lord's Supper with compulsory attendance except for the excommunicated, replaced Roman marriage law, and instituted a college of elders to implement church discipline. By mid-January 1537, the Large and Small Councils had accepted the *Articles*. However, they reduced the frequency of communion services to quarterly, rejected the notion of church discipline, and refused to require the taking of an oath. Calvin, who by now had begun preaching regularly on Sundays, worked with Farel to have the *Articles* fully accepted, in July persuading the Small Council to agree to exile those who would not take an oath accepting the confession of faith. In November a gathering of the *Conseil Générale* protested against the acceptance of even this limited form of the *Articles*, and in January 1538 the Council of Two Hundred also decided that no one should be excluded from communion.

This conflict took place against the background of accusations by Pierre Caroli, whom the Bernese council had appointed preacher in Lausanne in place of Viret, that Calvin's *Institutes* did not teach Trinitarian doctrine. Calvin was swift to defend himself, establishing good contacts with Bullinger in Zürich in the process. However, in the course of 1537 he found himself drawn into a conflict among the Bernese theologians which did nothing to improve his position in Geneva. By February 1538, when the elections of the new *syndics* took place, opposition to the methods of Calvin and Farel had grown to the extent that all those elected were opponents. The majority of the Small Council also stood against Calvin and Farel, rejecting their suggestions about church discipline and arguing that the civic authorities should exercise authority over the church. The council was determined not to lose control of the Reformation in their city. In March they explicitly required the preachers in Geneva to follow the church order and liturgical practices laid down in Bern, including the use of unleavened bread for communion, and the celebration of Christmas, New Year, the Annunciation, and the Ascension.

For Calvin, these questions were a matter for the church rather than the city council, which he referred to as the "council of the devil". He and Farel were told not to interfere in political matters, and were referred to the Bern city council for judgment. The Bernese authorities instructed them to use Bernese practices; an instruction which they ignored. On their return to Geneva, Calvin was incensed – and said so publicly – when the Small Council banned the elderly Élie Corault first from preaching and then, when he disobeyed, from Geneva. In response, the council instructed Calvin and Farel to celebrate Easter communion according to the Bernese Rite. Instead, they decided not to celebrate an Easter communion at all, "not because of the bread question, but because we would have defamed the sacrament by celebrating it with people who are so unworthy". On 23 April 1538, with the support of Geneva's citizens, the Small Council declared that divine services in Geneva should be conducted according to the rites and practices of Bern, and instructed Corault, Calvin and Farel to leave Geneva within three days. Guessing what was coming, they had not waited for the council's edict, but had left earlier that morning.

The shaping of a ministry: Calvin in Strasbourg (1538–41)
From Geneva, Calvin and Farel made their way to Basel, stopping en route in Bern to present a view of what had

transpired in Geneva, which was soon countered by reports from the Genevan city council. They had intended to travel on to Zürich, but changed their plans when Bullinger let it be known that he disapproved of how they had handled matters in Geneva. Calvin looked forward to a time of peace in which he could resume his studies. However, Martin Bucer was insistent that he go to Strasbourg, in part to separate him from Farel, whose influence Bucer felt to be unfortunate, but more importantly to offer lectures on the Bible and to act as pastor of the French exile congregation. Calvin declined the invitation, but when Bucer likened him to Jonah, fleeing before God's command to preach in the city of Nineveh, he gave in. On 8 September 1538, he preached his first sermon to the French congregation in Strasbourg.

Strasbourg was one of the most important free imperial cities in the Holy Roman Empire. As in Geneva, the second half of the fifteenth century had seen the city council beginning to assert its authority over against that of the bishop and chapter in a variety of areas relating to city life. The council had taken over responsibility for care of the sick from the religious orders, applying to the pope for permission to have an indulgence preached in order to raise funds to build a hospital in the city. Reform of the church had been called for in the late fifteenth century by Sebastian Brant and Jacob Wimpheling, humanist-inclined scholar-priests who urged the restoration of traditional Christianity purged of abuses. As early as 1478, the city council established the office of "cathedral preacher" to which it appointed Johann Geiler von Kaysersberg. He proved a popular and persuasive preacher, calling the people to amendment of life, exhorting the city's rulers to exercise their office according to Gospel principles, and instructing the clergy to abandon the trappings and behaviour of worldliness. Strasbourg's citizens took the rebuke to the clergy seriously, and were prepared to go to court to restrain clerical excess. In the winter of 1520–21, violent altercations took place in response to the behaviour of allegedly immoral clergy. A number of court cases were initiated by Strasbourg citizens seeking to take sanctions against clergy for engaging in immoral behaviour with daughters of the city. Long before the Reformation was officially introduced, steps had been taken in Strasbourg to reform the church.

Consequently, when Matthias Zell began to preach Luther's theology in Strasbourg, sometime in 1521, much of what he had to say resonated with the hopes and interests of the city and its council. The evangelical message was strengthened when in 1523 the Hebrew scholar Wolfgang Capito arrived in Strasbourg accompanied by his friend and student, the humanist Caspar Hedio. Soon afterwards, Martin Bucer returned to his native city, bringing with him his wife, the former nun Elisabeth Silbereisen. Bucer had been excommunicated by the Bishop of Speyer on account of his marriage, and the Bishop of Strasbourg sought to have him expelled from the city, but the city council granted him sanctuary on the basis of his citizenship. During the months that followed, Strasbourg's council assumed responsibility for care of the poor, took possession of monastic buildings (by 1526 most of Strasbourg's religious communities had been dispersed), and began to pay clerical salaries. In 1524, mass began to be celebrated in the cathedral using a German liturgy with communion being administered in both kinds. Soon the German liturgy, congregational singing and vernacular sermons were introduced at churches across the city. Strasbourg had become one of the earliest cities to embrace the Reformation, taking an approach that married together ecclesiastical and social reforms.

The central figure of Strasbourg's Reformation was Martin Bucer. Bucer was a humanist-educated former Dominican who had become attracted to Luther's ideas in 1518, when he heard him speak at the Heidelberg Disputation. By 1520 Bucer had been accused of teaching heresy by his superiors and had left his monastery. In 1521 he formally left the order and was appointed priest to the parish of Sickingen, only to be expelled from this post on his marriage a year later. Bucer was deeply impressed by Luther's theology. However, once he became active in Strasbourg, he discovered also a deep affinity to the approach to reform taken by Zwingli in Zürich. Both Zwingli and Bucer worked in cities in which the city council not only had a strong interest in ecclesiastical reform, but also expected to be closely involved in implementing it. They developed a shared conviction that the reform of theology and the church must be accompanied by reform of civic life, intended to assist the whole city to live in a more godly way. As the theological tensions between Luther and Zwingli became clear in the 1520s, Bucer sought to mediate between them.

Bucer's signature to the Marburg Articles stood in the list of Zwingli and his followers, but his aim was always to emphasize the common ground between Luther and Zwingli. He described the presence of Christ in the Eucharist as "sacramental", hoping that this terminology might make it possible to reconcile Luther's and Zwingli's positions. At the Diet of Augsburg in 1530, Bucer presented the *Confessio tetrapolitana* – the *Confession of the Four Cities* (the southern German cities Strasbourg, Constance, Lindau, and Memmingen) – a third statement of faith alongside the

Augsburg Confession presented by Philip Melanchthon on behalf of Luther, and Zwingli's *Account of the Faith*. Strasbourg was positioning itself in a southern German block, allied to but different from northern German reform. However, by the mid-1530s, the leaders of reform in Strasbourg had realized the political necessity of entering into an alliance with Wittenberg in order that they might join the Schmalkaldic League. Moreover, while Bucer had initially remained in close contact with Heinrich Bullinger in Zürich after Zwingli's death, by the mid-1530s the relationship between them had soured. Bucer and Capito entered into negotiations with the Wittenberg theologians which in 1536 resulted in the signing of the Wittenberg Concord, which marked a level of theological agreement between Bucer and Luther. In accepting Bucer's invitation to Strasbourg, Calvin was being given the opportunity to work with one of the most significant and influential German theologians, a man who had considerable experience of the practicalities of reform.

Strasbourg offered Calvin the experience of a secure Reformation, without the factions which had complicated relationships in Geneva. He gained pastoral, liturgical and leadership experience through his work with the French exile church, taking advantage of the opportunity of trying out his approach to ecclesiastical discipline in a congregation which was virtually independent of the political authorities. Calvin drafted French orders of service for holy communion, baptism and marriage; introduced into the services the singing of metrical psalms, of the *nunc dimittis* and of the Ten Commandments; instigated forms of public, communal confession of sins; and admitted no one to communion who had not first presented themselves to the ministers for examination.

At Strasbourg's Academy, he lectured on biblical exegesis and on specific biblical books, including the Gospel of John and First Corinthians, and prepared his *Commentary on Romans* for publication. In 1539, he published a second, much expanded version of the *Institutes*, which (he said in the new subtitle) he now believed to merit its title. A French version – not simply a translation, for Calvin was aware of the difference in educational background between those who could read Latin and those who read only French – appeared in 1541. At the request of the Genevan authorities, he wrote a response to the attempts of Cardinal Jacopo Sadoleto to persuade Geneva to return to the Roman church, which became one of the classic justifications of the necessity of the Reformation. In 1540, Calvin married Idelette de Bure, the widow of the Anabaptist Johann Stordeur.

Through the international engagement of Bucer and Capito, his time in Strasbourg also brought Calvin into contact with wider circles of reformers. Calvin attended the series of colloquies, or theological discussions, which took place during 1540 and 1541 at Hagenau, Worms, and in conjunction with the Imperial Diet at Regensburg. He signed the Augsburg Confession possibly in its original form of 1530 and certainly in the 1540 *variata* form revised by Melanchthon, hoping to gain the support of the German evangelical princes for Huguenots in France. Through his attendance at the colloquies, Calvin met and became friends with Philip Melanchthon. Calvin would later write a preface to the French translation of Melanchthon's theological textbook, the *Loci Communes*, and the two would correspond until Melanchthon's death in 1560.

Throughout this period, Calvin remained in contact with Geneva. The expulsion of Calvin and Farel had not brought peace among the different factions, and by 1540 those who had supported Calvin's ministry were beginning to gain the upper hand. Calvin began to receive requests from Geneva that he return, and by the autumn these had the express support of the Small Council. A deputation was sent from Geneva to Strasbourg to negotiate terms with him. Finding he had gone to Worms for the colloquy, it followed him there. From Regensburg, Calvin wrote to Farel that despite his reluctance he would return to Geneva. At the beginning of September, he set out from Strasbourg in the company of a mounted escort.

Calvin the reformer: The shaping of the Genevan church (1541–59)

The Genevan magistrates granted Calvin a substantial house near the cathedral and a salary of 500 florins, double that of the other pastors and more than that of most of the magistrates. This package of benefits would allow him to host students, churchmen, and other significant guests. Calvin sent for Idelette to join him and took up his preaching in the cathedral at the point where he had left off just before Easter 1538. This was not to be a new ministry, but a continuation of what he had started three years before.

In the weeks that followed his return, Calvin oversaw the drafting of a new church order which was passed by the Small Council on 27 September and by the General Council before the end of November. Calvin's *Ordonnances ecclésiastiques* (church ordinances) were intended to shape the religious, ecclesiastical, moral and social life of Geneva's citizens to that of a godly people. They envisioned four ranks of ministry, derived by Calvin from Paul's letters: the pastors, who were responsible for preaching, administering the sacraments, and the oversight of pastoral care; the doctors, theologians who were responsible for the education and teaching of both pastors and laity (Calvin, who was never ordained, viewed himself as belonging to this category); the twelve elders, chosen – at the council's insistence – from among the members of Geneva's councils (two from the Small Council, four from the Council of Sixty, and six from the Large Council), who were responsible for the life of the church and for church discipline; and the deacons, who carried out measures of practical pastoral care, including poor relief and care of the sick, under the supervision of the pastors. The pastors and doctors made up the Venerable Company (*vénérable compagnie*), presided over, until shortly before his death, by Calvin as its moderator. The Venerable Company ordered and taught doctrine, and selected pastors, who were then formally appointed by the city council. The pastors and elders formed the Consistory, presided over by one of the four *syndics,* which oversaw church discipline and regulated the conduct of Geneva's population. Together, the Venerable Company and the Consistory took over many of the ecclesiastical responsibilities previously exercised by the bishop. The 1541 *Ordonnances* reinstated geographically defined parishes which were responsible for administering baptism, catechism and holy communion to all those living within them.

The *Ordonnances* also made provision for a redefinition of the liturgical practices of the Genevan church. In 1542, Calvin issued a directory of worship, the "Form of prayers and singing and the manner of administering the sacraments and celebrating marriages on the basis of the customs of the Early Church." The focus was on a weekly pattern of preaching and teaching aimed at clergy and students but open to all. Wednesday was deemed a day of prayer, and attendance at the morning service was expected. Sunday was the day of prayer and rest. Again, attendance at the service – theoretically lasting one hour, but often much longer on account of the sermon – was expected of all. As in Strasbourg, which served as the model for much of Calvin's liturgical reform, men and women were expected to sit separately; vernacular psalms were sung in unison; and worshippers stood or sat, but did not kneel. In accordance with the focus on Sunday worship, the liturgical calendar was reduced to a minimum. Saints' days and festivals which did not fall on a Sunday were abolished. The council, however, insisted on reinstating the feasts of the Annunciation, the Circumcision of Christ, and Ascension, which were marked until 1545, and Christmas, which was celebrated until 1550, and thereafter kept on the nearest Sunday. Calvin objected in particular to the keeping of the Annunciation, which he saw as tending to sustain a problematic mariological piety; he would have preferred Good Friday to be kept in its stead.

The *Ordonnances* also required that children be taught the catechism. In 1542 Calvin revised the catechism he had drawn up in 1537 to produce what was effectively a new work in question-and-answer format divided into four major sections. The first, "Of Faith", explained the creed; the second, "Of the Law", the Ten Commandments, the use of the Law and the principles of neighbourly love; the third, "On Prayer", the Lord's Prayer; and the fourth, "On Sacraments", commented on baptism, the Eucharist, the office of the pastor, and church discipline. This revised Luther's order of the Ten Commandments, the creed followed by the Lord's Prayer, representing Calvin's conviction that God meant the Law not only to convict sinners of their sinfulness, but also to instruct believers in the godly life. It was required that the catechism be taught to the children of each parish on Sundays at noon, and parents were also expected to use it for teaching at home, thus educating the parents as well as the children. The 1542 Geneva Catechism became the most significant teaching document for the Reformed church in France. In Calvin's 1545 Latin translation, it shaped the Reformed catechetical tradition, including the influential Heidelberg Catechism of 1563.

The *Ordonnances* introduced ecclesiastical, liturgical, and moral reforms on a wide scale, seeking to codify and systematize the shape of the Reformation in Geneva. When they were presented to Geneva they represented a vision, rather than a depiction of reality. This was to some extent a question of personnel. French-speaking pastors educated in the correct interpretation of Scripture and the practices of the Reformation were central to the enacting of the *Ordonnances*. However, in the early 1540s, Geneva was desperately short of pastors. Unlike in most areas of Germany or German-speaking Switzerland, where the introduction of the Reformation often found considerable support among local clergy, many of whom soon became enthusiastic preachers of the evangelical Gospel, the introduction of the Reformation into Geneva had seen a disastrous fall in numbers of clergy. Pre-Reformation Geneva had enjoyed the services of more than 400 priests, monks and other members of religious orders (of whom more than 160 were associated with the cathedral). After the introduction of the Reformation, when the Catholic clergy and members of religious orders were told to leave Geneva, many of Geneva's rural parishes were left with no clergy at all, and only a handful remained in the city.

One of Calvin's priorities was to recruit educated French-speaking pastors and preachers who had experience of the Reformation, whom he could rely on to take the kind of lead he had envisaged when he set up the Venerable Company and the Consistory. By the mid-1540s, he had been successful, and the Venerable Company was made up primarily of his own compatriots.

The new four-fold shape of the ministry was not of itself controversial, but Calvin's vision of its relationship to the city authorities was. At stake was the balance of power between the temporal and spiritual authorities. Calvin believed that the *gouvernement spirituelle* should be independent. He wanted matters such as the appointment of ministers, decisions relating to the practical running of the church and the definition of doctrine and liturgical practice to be resolved by the Venerable Company, with appeal to the elders if necessary. The council wished to retain the power to choose and appoint pastors, and to cede only an advisory role to the Venerable Company, arguing that the church should be controlled by the temporal authorities, as in Bern or Zürich. The city council's insistence that elders should be drawn from their own ranks and that the council should appoint pastors was intended to counter this independence. In practice there was considerable personal overlap between the ministry of the church and membership of the council. The council also wished to retain the power of excommunication, which Calvin believed should be exercised by the Consistory. Calvin finally got his way in this matter in 1555. The assertion of the independence of the church from the temporal authorities was fundamental to Calvin's understanding of the church and its relationship with the state.

In the years to come, Calvin's strongly held theological views would shape – and sour – his relationships with many of Geneva's leading citizens. Sebastian Castellio, rector of Geneva's high school or *Gymnasium*, resigned in 1544 on account of his differences with Calvin over the canonical nature of the Song of Songs, and his rejection of Calvin's interpretation of what it meant to say that after his death Christ *descensit ad inferos*. As he had explained in the 1536 edition of the *Institutes*, Calvin understood this to mean that Christ "descended into hell ... and felt the dread and severity of divine judgment" (reading the text *descensit ad infernas*), while Castellio interpreted it to mean that Christ "descended to the dead". In 1546, Pierre Ameaux, a member of the Small Council and maker of playing cards who was involved in a complex divorce case, was sentenced to public penance for criticizing Calvin during a private dinner. A former monk, Jacques Gruet, was tried and executed in 1547 for blasphemy and political conspiracy after he published pamphlets criticizing Calvin. Jerome Bolsec, a surgeon who preached against the doctrine of predestination, was arrested and in 1551 banned for life. Perhaps most notoriously, the Spanish exile and anti-Trinitarian Michael Servetus, who had fled to France from the Inquisition in Italy in 1553, went to Geneva where he was arrested, tried and sentenced to death by burning. Calvin and the city council were prepared to take strong measures to ensure the stability of their Reformation.

Geneva's political situation became more stable in 1549, when Calvin and Bullinger signed the *Consensus Tigurinus* (Zürich Agreement). This allied Geneva and Zürich not only theologically, but to some extent politically. Calvin had high hopes that Lutherans would also sign it, but instead the

Consensus not only alienated the Lutherans but also caused problems with other Swiss cities, including Bern and Basel.

It was not until 1555 that Calvin and his supporters were finally firmly in control in Geneva. In 1558 the Genevan Academy was established as an educational institution for Reformed theology. Its first rector was Theodore Beza, and it attracted students from across Europe. While the German territories continued to teeter on the brink of bitter and violent territorial and religious disputes, Geneva became an international centre for the Reformation.

CHAPTER 4

CALVIN'S THEOLOGY

Unlike Luther, Calvin was drawn into an evangelical movement which had already taken shape in particular ways. His theology and his vision of the church were to be highly influential on that movement, but he was aware that he was building on foundations which Luther and others had laid. Calvin always saw Luther as a leader of the Reformation movement. As he wrote to the emperor Charles V in 1544: "God raised up Luther and others, who held forth a torch to light us into the way of salvation, and who, by their ministry, founded and reared our churches." Calvin was also influenced by the French humanist reform movement which had brought him to the Reformation, and by the work of reformers in other parts of Germany and Switzerland, especially Martin Bucer in Strasbourg, the legacy of Huldrych Zwingli (whom he never met), and the ongoing work of Heinrich Bullinger in Zürich, and by his contacts to (and conflicts with) reformers in Basel and Berne. Although he developed – and defended – distinctive theological views of his own, Calvin also saw himself as a mediator between different strands of the Reformation.

Calvin's theology was forged through his study of Scripture and the Church Fathers, his preaching and teaching, and his experiences in Strasbourg and Geneva. His sermons and his biblical commentaries were the means through which he worked out his theology. However, he also laid out his theological convictions in his famous work *Institutiones christianae religionis*, the *Institutes,* or *Institutions* – meaning "principles of instruction", or "principles of arrangement" – *of the Christian Religion.* This was a much more systematic work than Luther ever produced, and the different editions allow Calvin's developing theology to be traced.

In the subtitle to the first edition of the *Institutes*, published in 1536, Calvin explained that he saw his work as "embracing almost the whole sum of piety and whatever is necessary to know the doctrine of salvation". This first edition took the form of a catechetical work, intended, as we have seen above, to inform and instruct his countrymen.

After the dedicatory epistle, Calvin's work followed a similar structure to Luther's *Large Catechism*, which was certainly an important influence. Calvin considered Law, focusing on an exposition of the Ten Commandments; faith, with an explanation of the Apostles' Creed; prayer, based on an exposition of the Lord's Prayer; the sacraments, baptism and the Eucharist, with a rejection of the "false sacraments" (confirmation, penance, extreme unction "as they call it", ordination and marriage); and finally three themes which would become central to his thought: Christian freedom, ecclesiastical power, and the relationship of the Christian to the political administration. This was quite a small book, designed to introduce the reader to the evangelical faith as Calvin understood it. It was also an apologetic work, defending his position against those who disagreed. Through the re-workings that followed in the course of Calvin's career, the *Institutes* continued to preserve a balance between the systematic presentation of theological ideas, pastoral instruction and apologetics.

By the time Calvin came to publish the second Latin edition of the *Institutes* in 1539, he could draw on his experience of his first period in Geneva. In this edition he gave more attention to the doctrine of justification by faith, and for the first time devoted a section to the question of election and predestination. The second edition also saw the emergence of several themes which are often seen as characteristic of Calvin's theology: the relationship between the Old and New Testaments; the inter-connection between predestination and providence; a more developed understanding of the sacraments, and particularly the Eucharist; and a strong emphasis on the Christian life.

While in Strasbourg, Calvin prepared an edition of the *Institutes* in French, which was published in 1541. This was a translation and adaptation of the 1539 edition, explicitly intended for an audience needing theological instruction in the vernacular. The 1541 *Institutes* was the first major theological work to appear in French. Calvin had to craft the language in which it was written. The challenges were not simply linguistic. He was well aware that those who could read his works only in French would have a different educational and theological background than his Latin readers, and he wanted to make what he wrote accessible to them. His experience of ministry to the French exile congregation in Strasbourg informed his efforts to make his theological programme accessible to those with no formal Latin or theological education.

Calvin continued to work on the *Institutes* after his return to Geneva. A third major Latin edition was published between 1543 and 1545. The final Latin edition appeared in 1559; the final French edition in 1560. This edition had a completely new structure of four books: "Of the knowledge of God the Creator"; "Of the knowledge of God the Redeemer, in Christ, as first manifested to the Fathers under the Law, and thereafter to us under the Gospel"; "The mode of obtaining the Grace of Christ, the benefits it confers, and the effects resulting from it" (concerned with justification); and "Of the external means or helps by which God allures us into fellowship with Christ, and keeps us in it" (concerned with the church, the sacraments, and the temporal estate). The final edition of *Institutes* reveals the priorities and preoccupations of the theology which Calvin had worked out in his preaching and teaching, and in discussion and debate with others.

Grace, justification, and predestination

Calvin's theology is often characterized as placing an even stronger emphasis on predestination or, as he preferred to call it, election. However, while the doctrine of divine election was important for Calvin, his understanding of election can only be properly understood in the context of his strong emphasis on grace. This in turn is rooted in his understanding of the relationship between God and fallen humankind. Calvin, like Luther, was utterly convinced that justification could come about only through faith, and that faith must be a gift of God's grace. It is the overwhelming sense of God's grace, rather than the doctrine of election itself, which is the focus of Calvin's theology.

As he made clear in the final edition of the *Institutes*, Calvin developed his ideas about election – the idea that it is God who decides who is saved and who is damned – in response to the question of why, when the Gospel is preached, it is not heard in the same way by everyone, so that God's Word "does not gain the same acceptance either constantly or in equal degree". He maintained that the response of each individual person to the Gospel must be God's choice. Like Luther in his debate with Erasmus, Calvin understood the doctrine of election as a logical consequence of justification by faith. Since "our salvation comes about solely from God's generosity" and "every part of our salvation rests with Christ that we may glory in the Lord alone" it must be God who chooses who is to partake of grace. In Calvin's view, no one can ever deserve grace, for the true state of humankind is "to be on so many counts liable before God's judgment seat that challenged on a thousand points they cannot give satisfaction even on one". This realization should serve simply to increase gratitude for the undeserved gift of God's grace to those who receive it. For Calvin, the doctrine of election is an expression of the true nature of God's overwhelming grace.

God's gift of grace to fallen humanity formed the foundation of Calvin's theology. In the opening words of the *Institutes*, from the first edition, he affirmed: "Nearly all the wisdom we possess, that is to say, true and sound wisdom, consists of two parts: the knowledge of God and of ourselves." In 1536, he moved from these opening words to contrast the nature of God – "infinite wisdom, righteousness, goodness, mercy, truth, power and life", the source of all goodness – with the state of fallen human nature which has "lost all the benefits of divine grace" and become "far removed from God" and "a complete stranger". By 1541, these words led into opening sections exploring knowledge of God (inasmuch as this is humanly possible) and knowledge of humankind, including free will. In the first, he emphasized the way in which "we are born for the purpose of knowing God". In the second, he focused on humanity's utter need for God's intervention, concluding:

> The human understanding is so completely separated from God's righteousness that it cannot imagine, conceive or understand anything at all except all wickedness, sin, and corruption; similarly that the human heart is so much poisoned with sin that it can only produce corruption.

In the 1559 edition Calvin explained that "quite clearly, the mighty gifts with which we are endowed are hardly from ourselves; indeed, our very being is nothing but subsistence in the one God". All that we are and all that we have comes from God. Indeed, "our very poverty better discloses the infinitude of benefits reposing in God". Calvin's characteristic focus that human beings can only do good with God's help is very clear.

If all that we have comes from God, what does it mean for us to be justified? In the first edition of the *Institutes*, Calvin wrote of the importance of the desire to be justified in language somewhat reminiscent of Erasmus's: "If we implore [God's] helping hand, surely we will be persuaded that, equipped with his protection, we will be able to do all things." Human beings cannot fulfil what God requires: "There is no-one of us with either the will or the ability to do his duty." For Calvin, as for

Luther, the law existed to make this clear. It is "a mirror for us wherein we may discern and contemplate our sin and curse, just as we commonly gaze upon the scars and blemishes of our face in a mirror". For Calvin, again as for Luther, it was only when we have reached this point of despair in our own capabilities that we understand our need of God, a need to which God responds: "After we descend to this humility and submission, the Lord will shine upon us, and show himself lenient, kindly, gentle, indulgent."

Grace is a gift of God, but in the first edition of the *Institutes* Calvin seemed to suggest that God's gift of grace is to some extent a response to human longing or prayer: "if we implore [God's] helping hand" or "if we pray to him to avert his wrath, he will without a doubt grant it to us". Nonetheless, Calvin also acknowledged that God's will is paramount: "He bestows on us according to his own good will a new heart, in order that we may will, and a new power, whereby we may be enabled to carry out his commandments [Ezek. 36:26]." God's gifts and benefits, "which include free forgiveness of sins, peace and reconciliation with God, the gifts and graces of the Holy Spirit" are ours, argued Calvin, "if we embrace and receive them with sure faith, utterly trusting God, not doubting that God's Word, which promises us all these things, is power and truth". There was for Calvin at this stage a sense of a need for active acceptance of grace by the human heart, for giving ourselves to God, rather as is found in Luther's *Large Catechism*, or in Erasmus's work *On Free Will*. And yet, Calvin also emphasized that this faith is "not from ourselves"; rather, "It is God who is to be asked to lead us, unfeignedly repentant, to knowledge of ourselves; to lead us, by sure faith, to the knowledge of his greatness and of his sweetness." The relationship between

God's gift of grace and the human response was worked out through his later theology.

When he reworked the *Institutes* in 1539, Calvin introduced sections on penitence, on justification by faith and the merit of works, and on predestination and providence. His understanding of predestination was rooted in his understanding of justification by faith. He explained:

> That person is said to be justified before God, who is counted righteous before God's judgment and is acceptable to His righteousness. That person is said to be justified by faith who, being excluded from the righteousness of works, by faith grasps Jesus Christ's righteousness and, clad in that, appears before God's face not as a sinner but as righteous.

Believers will come before God in utter humility, knowing themselves to be "completely empty and poor" and giving themselves entirely to God's mercy. In doing so, they will turn to Christ: "If we seek salvation, life and immortality, we must have recourse nowhere else, since Christ alone is the fountain of life, the door of salvation, and the heir of the heavenly kingdom." For Calvin, this realization was the content of faith – but it was also the content of election. We may think of ourselves as turning to God, but in reality it is God who gives us faith and draws us to him, so that "we, being adopted by God as His children, may obtain salvation and immortality in His grace and love". This implies election by God. No one can choose to be adopted by God; God must choose them.

In expounding the doctrine of predestination, the key question for Calvin was pastoral. Why is it that not everyone who hears the Word of God preached responds in faith? His response was that faith must be given by God, for it is God's illumination: "When God's mercy is presented to both the faithful and the unbelievers by the gospel, it is only faith, that is, God's illumination, which may distinguish between them so that the faithful sense the efficaciousness of the gospel, but the unbelievers get no good from it." In the 1539/41 *Institutes*, the doctrine of election was closely linked to Calvin's conviction of God's providence, the ongoing, continuing care for the world. For Calvin, God's involvement with the world was such that God "with wisdom directs and disposes each thing to its end". Predestination was at one with Calvin's affirmation of God's intimate involvement in the events of the world.

In the 1559 edition of the *Institutes*, Calvin integrated his discussion of predestination into his presentation of justification in Book Three. Calvin's question in this book was how the benefits of Christ, which he had explored in Book Two, might be received. He concluded that it is the Holy Spirit who builds the relationship between the believer and Christ. For this, faith, given to the believer by God, is necessary. This faith, Calvin explained, "rests not on ignorance, but on knowledge"; we believe "when we know that God is our merciful Father, because of reconciliation effected through Christ, and that Christ has been given to us as righteousness, sanctification, and life". Faith, he noted, is not about "submitting your feelings obediently to the church", but neither is it about a purely intellectual knowledge. Rather, it is "a knowledge of God's will toward us, perceived from his Word". It is God's Word which testifies "that our salvation is [God's] care and concern" and through which we receive "the promise of grace, which can testify to us that the Father is merciful". That faith is given by God, on God's decision, made before the beginning of the world. There is no other way to approach God for, as Calvin beautifully put it, "Upon grace alone the heart of man can rest."

Reason, revelation, and knowledge of God

In contrast to his pessimistic view of the faculties of fallen humankind, Calvin had a positive conception of human capabilities before the fall. His explication "Of the knowledge of God" in the 1539/41 edition of the *Institutes* demonstrated the dramatic curtailing of the human ability to know God. Human beings, for Calvin, were created to know God: "Let us take it as beyond doubt that there is in the human spirit a natural inclination, some feeling of divinity." The existence of this "seed of religion" was for Calvin what rendered culpable the human failure to accord God the worship due to him. If human beings were not made to know God, then they would not be sinful if they did not know him. Even in their attempts to know God, however, the "seed of religion" shows itself to be corrupted. As a result, people tend to seek God within their own understanding: "They do not understand Him at all as He has given Himself to be known, but imagine Him as they have made Him by their presumption." The effect of this was to make a god of human imaginings or of human practices, so that people paid lip service to religious observance driven by fear, while not amending their lives. In contrast, "The faithful heart ... does not attribute to Him what it pleases but is satisfied to have Him as He reveals Himself." For Calvin, God revealed himself not in the fullness of his self, but "in such a fashion as is necessary for us to know Him for our salvation". That is, God accommodates himself to the capability of human senses and of human understanding.

One important means of such revelation is the natural world. Calvin was convinced that the natural world, because it had been created by God, was also capable of revealing God. As he affirmed in the 1539/41 *Institutes*, and reiterated in the 1559 edition:

> No matter which way you turn your eyes, there is no part of the world so small that at least some spark of His glory does not shine there. Particularly, you cannot look around and contemplate this beautiful masterpiece of the whole world in its breadth and width, without (in a manner of speaking) being completely blinded by the infinite abundance of light.

Consequently, "there are endless proofs in both heaven and earth which bear witness to [God's] amazing wisdom". Human reason provided the means of understanding these, particularly in the case of those matters "which are difficult to comprehend and which can be understood only by the means of astronomy, medicine, and physics". Education was useful here. However, Calvin noted that even people who are not educated in the liberal arts can still see "much skill and cleverness in God's works". In the 1539/41 *Institutes*, Calvin wanted to affirm that those educated in the liberal arts "have a special help for entering more profoundly into contemplation of the secrets of the divine wisdom", although he also thought that even the most untutored person could recognize "the superiority of divine wisdom" in the number and order of the stars or in the "unity, proportion, beauty, and usefulness" of the human body, as demonstrated by Galen. Similarly, God's powers could be recognized in his providential works, and in the way that God directs and governs the world.

Nonetheless, Calvin argued, human faculties can never be enough to understand truly what is revealed. These "lamps in the edifice of the world, shining to illuminate the Creator's glory for a person" cannot actually lead us in the right path. Calvin did believe that "the invisible divinity is represented by the form of the world" but, because of the fallen state of human beings, and because of the distance between human beings and God, he added a caveat: "Our eyes fail to see that divinity unless they are illuminated through faith." By the time he published the 1559 *Institutes*, Calvin had come to the conclusion that in "physics, dialectics, mathematics and other like disciplines" God's gift is "freely offered". However, it is incomplete "when a solid foundation of truth does not underlie it". The inability of philosophers to agree was for Calvin a witness to the inability of fallen human nature reliably to interpret the revelation which had been offered. The result, he concluded, was a "boundless filthy mire of error" which filled the whole world. Calvin therefore left the faithful with an insoluble conundrum: "Although we lack the natural ability to mount up to the pure and clear knowledge of God, all excuse is cut off because the fault of dullness lies within us." After the fall, "something of understanding and judgment remains a residue" and "in man's perverted and degenerate nature some sparks still gleam". Human beings were thus seen to be rational beings, "differing from brute beasts" and yet "they show this light choked with dense ignorance, so that it cannot come forth effectively". Although Calvin believed God to offer myriad testimonies which could reveal him, he also believed that human beings would not understand these correctly, but would always be misled by their corrupt reason. True knowledge of God the creator could, therefore, in Calvin's view, only be attained through Scripture.

Revelation of Christ through Scripture was thus the only way of knowing God. For Calvin, Scripture was the basis of all knowledge of God, of the church and of all doctrine. He maintained that the church could not define the correct interpretation of Scripture. On the contrary, a true reading of Scripture must provide the foundation for the church and for its teaching, for "credibility of doctrine is not established until we are persuaded beyond doubt that God is its author". This conviction, he argued, would be found "in a higher place than human reasons, judgments or conjectures, that is, in the secret testimony of the Holy Spirit". For Calvin, Word and Spirit always belonged together. He rejected the idea that God might speak through the direct revelation of the Spirit without scriptural support. Rather, God "sent down the Spirit by whose power he had dispensed the Word, to complete his work by the efficacious confirmation of the Word". The Holy Spirit is both the author of Scripture and the mediator of true scriptural interpretation. It is through Scripture that knowledge of God as both Creator and Redeemer is attained.

As has already been seen, for Calvin, as for Luther, knowledge of the Redeemer cannot be attained by human free will. Redemption is a matter for God; for the human will, after the fall, was "so bound to wicked desires that it cannot strive after the right". Fallen human beings could, in Calvin's view, do nothing but choose the sinful. It was only when grace was at work in the human heart that the will could be converted to the good, for then God's will became the guide: "Nothing good can arise out of our will until it has been reformed; and after its reformation, in so far as it is good, it is so from God, not from ourselves." Calvin believed that it was God's action in instilling grace into a person's heart that made it possible for them to believe.

Calvin thought that this was shown by the Law. Initially his treatment of the Law was relatively brief, and formed a prelude and postlude to his exposition of the Ten Commandments. The Law, he wrote in 1536,

> teaches us God's will, which we are constrained to fulfil and to which we are in debt. ... It is a mirror for us wherein we may discern and contemplate our sin and curse, just as we commonly gaze upon the scars and blemishes of our face in a mirror.

This resonated with Luther's insistence that the Law convicts us of our sin – a position with which Calvin agreed. In 1559, he asserted that an awareness of sin could turn the sinner outside themselves and highlight the human need for God: "The miserable ruin, into which the rebellion of the first man cast us, especially compels us to look upward." This was a result of knowledge of the Law and particularly of the realization that we cannot fulfil it. In 1536, he asserted that "since it is not in our power or ability to discharge what we owe the law, we must despair of ourselves and must seek and await help from another quarter" – namely the Lord – who "will shine upon us and show himself lenient, kindly, gentle, indulgent" to those who show humility and submit themselves to him. The Law, for Calvin, would impel the unbeliever to an awareness of his or her need of God.

However, Calvin also saw a more positive aspect to the Law. As he noted in 1536, "This very written law is but a witness of natural law, a witness which quite often arouses our memory and instils in us the things we had not sufficiently learnt, when natural law was teaching us within." His conviction that the

Law also had a positive function would lead him from the beginning to expound, not two uses of the Law, as Luther did, but three: the theological or pedagogical use, in which the Law demonstrates the need for grace; the political or civic use, in which the Law lays down punishments for wrongdoings, controls malefactors, and thus orders society; and the third, normative or didactic, use, for "believers and those in whose hearts the Spirit of God already lives and reigns", who from the Law "learn more thoroughly each day what the Lord's will is like". By the second edition of the *Institutes*, Calvin was describing the third use of the Law as the "principle use, which pertains more closely to the proper purpose of the law". Unlike Luther, Calvin was adamant that God's Law pertained to believers and the justified, and could provide them with a proper rule of life.

While Calvin followed Luther in arguing that the Law demonstrated human sinfulness and showed the necessity of grace, it is apparent that he assigned the Law a more significant role in the life of the believer – of the regenerate or "reborn" – than did Luther. This was coupled with a more positive understanding of the salvific promises encapsulated in the Law. As contained in the Law, they were, in Calvin's view, vain, but they nonetheless pointed to the fullness of God's salvation. Through grace, he asserted in the final edition of the *Institutes*, the believer would receive the benefits promised by God in the Law:

> Even if the promises of the law, in so far as they are
> conditional, depend on perfect obedience to the law – which
> can nowhere be found – they have not been given in vain.
> For when we have learned that they will be fruitless and

ineffectual for us unless God, out of his free goodness, shall receive us without looking at our works, and we in faith embrace that same goodness held forth to us by the gospel … the Lord … causes us to receive the benefit of the promises of the law as if we had fulfilled their condition.

In consequence, Calvin did not follow Luther in seeing a stark opposition between Law and Gospel. Rather, the Gospel enabled the fulfilment of the promises offered in the Law, just as the covenant of the Old Testament was fulfilled – and not superseded – by that of the New Testament. Calvin thus saw more continuity between Law and Gospel, and between Old and New Testaments than did Luther. Indeed, Calvin refuted those – presumably including Luther – who, he said, "always erroneously compare the law with the gospel by contrasting the merit of works with the free imputation of righteousness". Law, he wrote in 1559, was "the rule of righteous living by which God requires of us what is his own". It was required of all: believers and unbelievers alike.

The church and the sacraments

One of Calvin's major contributions to Reformation theology is his doctrine of the church. His thought in this area took two decades to mature. It developed throughout his career, taking its final shape in the 1559 edition of the *Institutes*. Challenged by Cardinal Jacopo Sadoleto in March 1539 to defend his Reformation programme, Calvin began to articulate his understanding of the true church. In the 1539/41 editions of the *Institutes*, he devoted a chapter to discussing the power of the church. By the 1559 edition, his consideration of "the external means or aids by which God invites us into the society of Christ and holds us therein" had come to make up the whole of the fourth book, which was focused largely on the church and the sacraments. For Calvin, the church – characterized by true preaching and hearing of the Word of God and the proper administration of the sacraments – was the primary external means through which internal change and the reception of grace became possible.

Calvin's definition of the church drew on Article VII of the Augsburg Confession, written by Philip Melanchthon in 1530: "The Church is the congregation of saints, in which the Gospel is rightly taught and the Sacraments are rightly administered." In 1536, in the context of his exposition of the creed, he affirmed, in words which he would continue to use in every edition of the *Institutes*, "Wherever we see the Word of God purely preached and heard, where we see the sacraments administered according to Christ's institution, there, it is not to be doubted, the Church of God exists." The church of which he spoke was that which is concerned with "the administration of the Word of God", for "the Lord does not recognize anything of His own in any place except where His word is heard and reverently kept". Calvin rejected any idea that the Roman hierarchy could define what the church was or what it should believe, although at the same time he affirmed the authority of those pastors whose "whole office is limited to the administration of God's word, their whole wisdom to the knowledge of that word, and their whole eloquence to the preaching of that word". Here Calvin's clear distinction between the responsibilities of the church and those of the magistrates began to become apparent.

Calvin was dealing here with the visible church. As he recognized in the 1559 *Institutes*, in its true meaning, the church was made up of those "who are children of God by grace of adoption and true members of Christ by sanctification of the Holy Spirit". The true membership of the church of the elect was in Calvin's view unknown or invisible to those living on earth. The visible church, on the other hand, was made up of "the whole multitude of men spread over the earth who profess to worship one God and Christ". Membership of the visible church was marked by initiation through baptism, by partaking of the Eucharist which attests "our unity in true doctrine and love", and by agreement in understanding and preaching the Word of God. However, Calvin noted, "in this church are mingled many hypocrites who have nothing of Christ but the name and outward appearance", who were tolerated either because the church's discipline was not strong enough, or because no one was able to pass judgment over them. The visible church, for this reason, was always going to be imperfectly holy, "mingled of good men and bad", and it was necessary to bear with these imperfections. Those who sought to constitute a perfect church, Calvin suggested, were seeking a perfection which was not promised in this life. This was not to suggest that false preaching should be borne. There were false churches, among which Calvin numbered both the Roman church and the Anabaptists. Calvin's doctrine of the visible church showed him keenly aware of the need to acknowledge human weakness and fallibility.

For Calvin, one of the ways by which the visible church could be recognized was the proper administration of the sacraments. Like other reformers, he recognized only two: the Eucharist and baptism. His theology of the sacraments, and particularly of the Eucharist, sought to bridge the differences between the Lutheran and the Zwinglian positions. However,

Calvin's attempts to mediate were of no avail, and in 1549 he signed the *Consensus Tigurinus* (Zürich Agreement) with Heinrich Bullinger, Zwingli's successor in Zürich. His Eucharistic theology was rejected by the Lutheran Joachim Westphal, and this divide caused a lasting division between the churches of the Reformation.

In the first edition of the *Institutes*, Calvin described the sacraments as a means by which "God provides for the ignorance of our mind and for the weakness of our flesh". A sacrament, as an outward sign of the testimony of God's grace, is "joined to [God's promise] by way of an appendix, to confirm and seal the promise itself, and make it … more evident to us". Sealing would become one of Calvin's favoured metaphors for the effect of sacraments. As he explained in words which would appear in every edition of the *Institutes*, "The seals attached to government documents and other public acts are nothing taken by themselves, for they would be attached in vain if the parchment had nothing written on it. Yet, added to the writing, they do not on that account fail to confirm and seal what is written."

In this, Calvin was closer to Zwingli than to Luther. The sacraments, he thought, "are exercises which make us more certain of the trustworthiness of God's word" and that Word has already been heard. To some extent, Calvin shared Zwingli's conviction that the sacraments were a kind of badge of membership for those united in faith. In the *Consensus Tigurinus*, he agreed that the sacraments were "marks and badges of Christian profession and fellowship or fraternity". However, for Calvin they were more than this; through the sacraments, he believed, and the *Consensus Tigurinus* affirmed, God may "testify, represent, and seal his grace to us".

In some ways, however, Calvin's sacramental theology was closer to that of Luther than that of Zwingli. Calvin, unlike Zwingli, saw the sacraments as a means by which God might communicate the reality of the promise of salvation to human beings. By the time he came to revise the *Institutes* in 1539, he was pointing to the value of the physical reality of the sacraments: "They have the special trait, which is beyond the word, that they represent the promises visually, as if in a painting." They are the "pillars of our faith", resting on the foundation of God's Word; they offer "a mirror in which we can contemplate God's riches and grace". Indeed, they are a means by which God "manifests Himself to us in the way it is given to our dazed sense to be able to know Him". The sacraments, then, were a particular means of manifesting the Word to believers, and as such they were "witnesses of God's grace" and instruments of the assurance of God's blessing. And yet, although he affirmed that God could and did work through the sacraments to sustain faith, Calvin still insisted that a sacrament had no value in and of itself. God, he commented in 1559, "feeds our bodies through bread and other foods; he illuminates the world through the sun and warms it through its heat, yet neither bread, nor sun, nor fire, is anything save in so far as he distributes his blessings to us through these instruments". The power of the sacraments, he suggested in the 1539/41 *Institutes*, was simply the power of the Spirit "to engender, support, preserve and establish faith". The sacraments were of no use without the power of the Spirit.

Calvin's explanation of baptism in the 1536 edition of the *Institutes* indicated that he had already come to the conclusion that Zwingli's definition of the sacrament was inadequate. Baptism, he wrote, "was given to us by God: first, to serve our faith before him; secondly, to serve our confession before people". It could be said to serve our faith in that it was "a symbol of our cleansing ... a messenger sent to confirm to us that all our sins are so abolished ... that they can never come to [God's] sight". Baptism fortifies us for our life in Christ, even though we continuously fall away. And it reveals our new life in Christ, and the way that we share in Christ's blessings. None of this, he thought, should be taken to suggest that baptism could do away with original sin, for it could not. What was important for Calvin was the awareness of sin, for such an awareness indicated a deeper longing for unity with Christ: "Those who are disturbed, exercised, and pricked by their own flesh should not faint and be discouraged. Let them rather think that they are still on the road." The true fruits of baptism, Calvin emphasized, can never be achieved in this life, but can only be achieved in death, "when from this life we pass to the Lord". However, at the same time Calvin affirmed, with Zwingli, that baptism should also be understood as a confession of faith before others. He firmly resisted any suggestion that this implied that infants should not be baptized, arguing that infants "possess faith in common with adults" and that "all God's elect enter into eternal life through faith, at whatever point in age they are released from this prisonhouse of corruption". Baptism, in Calvin's eyes, served both to strengthen faith in Christ and to mark allegiance to Christ.

Calvin's understanding of baptism would not change significantly in the 1539/41 edition of the *Institutes*, although he offered much more extensive arguments against Anabaptists and those who rejected infant baptism, drawing on the parallel between infant baptism and circumcision (also used by Zwingli) and reiterating that the baptism of infants should be understood as a sign to the faithful. It served "to comfort the faithful person and give him courage to devote himself completely to God". Calvin was clear that children are capable of life in Christ, and if properly nurtured they would grow and mature into a full understanding of faith.

By the late 1540s, Calvin had come to see baptism additionally as "the sign of initiation by which we are received into the Church". His defence of infant baptism continued to be expanded, and in the final edition of the *Institutes* a whole chapter was dedicated to this question. He emphasized its benefits "both to the believers who present their children to be baptized, and to the infants themselves". Infant baptism for Calvin was an important affirmation of his conviction that God justifies by faith.

More controversial than baptism was the Eucharist. Calvin's exposition of the doctrine of the Eucharist in the 1536 *Institutes* had already indicated his familiarity with the whole gamut of contemporary understandings. He rejected a range of views: the medieval doctrine of transubstantiation; Luther's position that Christ's ascended body takes on the ubiquity of his divine nature; the idea that Christ's body is celestial in nature (a view probably held by the Schwenkfeldians and other so-called spiritualists); and the idea that the Eucharist cannot strengthen or sustain faith (perhaps the view of some Anabaptists).

Calvin's position affirmed the central importance of the Eucharist. Its "fruit of sweetness and comfort" is great, he wrote, for in it "we recognise Christ to have been so engrafted in us as we, in turn, have been engrafted in him, so that whatever is his we are permitted to call ours, whatever is ours to reckon as his". The Eucharist is thus a reminder of the truth upon which redemption is based: "… becoming Son of man with us, he has made us sons of God with him." Moreover, the parallel between physical eating and spiritual partaking of Christ was also important to Calvin: "… as bread nourishes, sustains and preserves the life of our body, so Christ's body is the food and protection of our spiritual life." The Eucharist manifested God's promise of salvation in such a perfect way "that we must truly consider [Christ] truly shown to us". However, it could be said not only to exhibit that promise to us, but also to draw us into it, and strengthen us in it. For Calvin, the heated discussions about the question of how Christ was present in the Eucharist had missed the point. Christ's ascended human body, he agreed with Zwingli, was in heaven, but since the power of the kingdom is "neither bounded by any location in space nor circumscribed by any limits" Christ was able to act where he willed:

> Uncircumscribed, Christ can exert his power wherever he pleases, in heaven and on earth; he can show his presence in power and strength; he is always able to be among his own people to live in them, sustain them, quicken, preserve them, as if he were present in the body.

Calvin conceded that this understanding of the Eucharist denied any physical presence of Christ in the elements: "We obviously mean that the very substance of his body or the true and natural body of Christ is not given there; but all those benefits which Christ has supplied us with in his body." Christ's ascended human body must be at the right hand of God, but this did not preclude the true benefits of union with Christ from being accessible through receiving the bread and wine at the Eucharist.

In later editions of the *Institutes*, Calvin expanded his understanding of Christ's presence, affirming more strongly that Christ's human body was in heaven, and invoking the doctrine of the Holy Spirit to explain Christ's presence in the Eucharist. Thus in the 1539/41 *Institutes*, he wrote:

> We must not imagine this communication to be the way the sophists have dreamed: as if the body of Christ descended onto the table and were set there in local presence to be touched with the hands, chewed with teeth, and swallowed up in the stomach. For we do not doubt that [Christ's body] has its own (finite) limits as the nature of a human body requires, and that body is contained in heaven where it was received until He will come for judgement. ... Therefore the bond of this joining is the Holy Spirit, by whom we are united together, and He is like a canal or channel by which all that Christ is and possesses comes down to us.

The Holy Spirit, Calvin would affirm in 1559, "truly unites things separated in space". It is not that Christ comes down to the believer in the bread, but that the community of believers are lifted to him. This, for Calvin, was the true meaning of what Christ commanded: "In his Sacred supper he bids me take, eat, and drink his body and blood under the symbols of bread and wine. I do not doubt that he himself truly presents them, and that I receive them."

Calvin saw the Eucharist as having many benefits. Most importantly, it strengthened faith. Secondly, as he pointed out in 1536, it called those who partook of it to proclaim and give thanks for the benefits they had received through Christ's death: "... to declare Christ's death until he come."

Thirdly, it exhorted those who received it to unity with Christ and with one another, through a growing awareness that all were members of one body "and that as no part of our body is touched by any feeling of pain which is not spread among the rest, so we ought not to allow a brother to be affected by any evil, without being touched by compassion for him".

In Calvin's view, one consequence of this understanding of the benefits of the Eucharist was that it should be received frequently. He rejected the idea that the Eucharist should be received only annually, arguing that it should be celebrated and received frequently, preferably at least once a week, in both kinds. He was convinced, however, that the benefits of the Eucharist would accrue only to those who partook of it in faith and worthily. For those who did not, it is "turned into deadly poison". Calvin was deeply exercised by what it meant for someone to eat worthily. He saw the admission of only those worthy to the Eucharist as in part the church's responsibility, and this was an important aspect of his understanding of the church's responsibility for discipline.

Church and state

In 1520, Luther had called upon princes and magistrates to reform the church. Although by the mid-1520s Luther envisaged a clear delineation between the responsibilities of the magistrate and those of the church, in practice the Lutheran Reformation continued to be shaped by princes and city councils who saw the spiritual lives of their subjects as their responsibility. Calvin had suffered from precisely this kind of attitude. In France he had experienced persecution of the church by the king and the state authorities, encouraged by the ecclesiastical hierarchy in the shape of the Sorbonne. In his first period in Geneva he had had his plans for reform rejected by the city council, and had left before he could be expelled. In Strasbourg he had witnessed the city council seeking to control the reforms initiated by Martin Bucer and the other Strasbourg reformers. His return to Geneva was shaped by his attempts – only partially successful – to wrest control of the church from the council. Luther's ideal of the separate responsibilities of the spiritual and temporal powers was an important influence on Calvin's strongly held belief that the church and the state had largely separate responsibilities. The kind of theocracy envisaged by Zwingli, in which the city council and the church were entirely integrated with one another, held no attraction for Calvin, although it held considerable attraction for Geneva's council. Calvin's theology of the relationship between church and state was forged in the crucible of these experiences and the struggle first to gain, and then to maintain, control over the church in Geneva.

Like Luther, Calvin argued in 1536 that "there is a two-fold government in man: one aspect is spiritual, whereby the conscience is instructed in piety and in reverencing God; the second is political, whereby man is educated for the duties of humanity and civil life". The first of these was the so-called spiritual jurisdiction or kingdom; the second, the temporal jurisdiction or political kingdom. Calvin suggested that the first was an internal matter, which "resides in the mind with us"; this was the jurisdiction of the church. The second was external; it "regulates only outward behaviour", by which Calvin meant that it dealt with "the concerns of the present life – not only with food and clothing but with laying down laws whereby a man may live his life among other men honourably and temperately". These responsibilities included also the defence of property, the preservation of the public peace, and the ensuring of a place for public religion, including the prevention of "idolatry, sacrilege against God's name, blasphemy against his truth, and other public offences against religion". However, Calvin also emphasized that he did not allow magistrates or anyone else "to make laws according to their own decision concerning religion and the worship of God". These must be made by the church on the basis of Scripture. The temporal jurisdiction created space for public religion and policed the boundaries of truth as defined by the religion. What it did not do was seek to define religious truth itself.

One important consequence of the distinction between spiritual and temporal jurisdictions for Calvin, as it had been for Luther, was that it ensured spiritual equality. "It makes no difference what your constitution among men may be or under what nation's laws you live, since the Kingdom of Christ does not at all consist in these things." Any person, in any station of life, might be a member of Christ's kingdom and thus of the true church. On the other hand, this distinction did nothing to disorder the structures of society. Magistrates and rulers remained magistrates and rulers, given their power and, perhaps more significantly, their authority, by God.

Because of the corruption of fallen human nature – humankind is made up of "evil men" whose "insolence … is so great, their wickedness so stubborn" – Calvin believed a form of political government to be necessary to regulate and order life in this world. Indeed, such government should be understood to be part of the human condition: "If it is the Lord's will that we go as pilgrims upon the earth while we aspire to the true fatherland" – that is, the kingdom of God

– "and if the pilgrimage requires such helps, those who take them from man deprive him of his very humanity." For Calvin, this government had three parts: "… the magistrate, who is the protector and guardian of the laws; the laws, according to which he governs; the people, who are governed by the laws and obey the magistrate."

Calvin argued that the office of magistrates was ordained by God, and that magistrates should always be aware that they exercised justice as God's deputies. On account of human weakness, he suggested that it was "safer and more bearable for a number to exercise government, so that they may help one another, teach and admonish one another". The magistrates, he thought, were responsible for administering justice and keeping the peace, and because of this, both the use of punishment, including the death penalty, and the waging of war might be necessary. Moreover, the laws by which magistrates exercised power were also given by God. Christians could – and should – appeal to the law courts, but they should do so without hatred and not in a spirit of persecution. Most important for Calvin was the expectation that the Christian would obey the magistrate. This applied not only in the case of a magistrate who was "a father of this country, a shepherd of his people, guardian of the peace, protector of righteousness and avenger of innocence", but also in the case of wicked rulers who pursued their own interests or exploited their people. Calvin saw obedience even to unjust rulers as part of the discipline of the Christian life. Christians should not attempt to impose the right themselves, but should rely on God to act on their behalf. Only if the ruler sought to impinge on freedom of religious expression should they be resisted, and then only by those whose responsibility it was to take such action. Although he recognized that God could act also through unjust or ungodly rulers, Calvin's primary interest was to remind magistrates and princes that they acted on behalf of God, and that they should behave accordingly.

From Calvin to Calvinism and the Reformed tradition

Calvin developed his theology and helped to shape the Genevan church with one eye on the situation in France. Geneva soon became a key source of theological writings in French, intended to assist their readers in deepening their understanding of the theology of the Reformation, and in particular of Calvin's Reformation. However, although Calvin's thought and theology was central to the development of the structures of the Huguenot churches in France, he was not the only influence, and he was never a leader of the French church. Indeed, Calvin, although influential, was not a figurehead as Luther had been.

One reason for this was the changing political situation in Western Europe. In the 1540s and 1550s, as Calvin was establishing his position in Geneva, the German Empire descended into a war in which Saxony played a major role. Wittenberg, in the middle of the contested territory, was no longer an attractive place for budding Protestants to study. Geneva offered a convincing alternative. Protestant exiles, from Italy, from Mary Tudor's England, from Hungary, or from some of the German lands, and others who sought training in the theology and ecclesiology of the Reformation church, discovered Geneva to be a good place to congregate and share their experiences. Out of this range of influences emerged a Calvinist tradition of theology and church practice that looked to Calvin as a primary influence, but there also emerged a broader Reformed tradition, characterized by a strong focus on preaching the Word of God, by the simplicity of its worship and church buildings, and frequently by congregational or presbyterian church structures. Calvin's ideal that the church should govern itself in independence of state structures made his ecclesiology particularly attractive to ecclesiastical and political leaders who sought reform of the church in opposition to the wishes of monarchs or other rulers.

This did not mean that rulers might not be interested in Calvin's ideas. The first territory outside Geneva to adopt Calvinism was the Palatinate, whose ruler, the Elector Friedrich III, came to be convinced by Calvin's theology in the late 1550s, and introduced a Calvinist order for the church in 1561. The University of Heidelberg soon became famous for its Calvinist teaching, and the influential Heidelberg Catechism was published in 1563 under Friedrich's aegis. East Friesland and its capital Emden – known as the Geneva of the north – had significant numbers of Reformed Protestants by the mid-1540s. The regent, Countess Anna, made the territory effectively bi-confessional (Lutheran and Reformed) and tolerated other Protestant groups, such as Anabaptists. Through their decision to adopt the Reformed faith, Friedrich and Anna introduced into his territory a faith which was not legal in the German Empire. The Peace of Augsburg, agreed in 1555, recognized only the Lutherans' Augsburg Confession as a legal basis for Protestant religion. Followers of Calvin and other Reformed theologians would not achieve legal recognition in the German Empire until the Peace of Westphalia in 1648.

In England, the Zürich reformers, especially Heinrich Bullinger, were initially more influential than Calvin. However,

English translations of some of Calvin's sermons and short treatises began to be published in England as early as the mid-1540s. Although no English edition of the *Institutes* would appear until the 1580s, Calvin's theology was certainly being read – probably mainly in Latin – in England under Edward VI, and possibly earlier. Thomas Cranmer (Archbishop of Canterbury from 1533) owned a copy of the 1536 *Institutes*. Calvin's acquaintance with the Strasbourg reformer Martin Bucer and the Italian exile Peter Martyr Vermigli may have served as a link to England, especially once Bucer and Vermigli moved from Strasbourg to England at the invitation of Thomas Cranmer. Edwardian England was an extremely hospitable environment for the theological ideas and practices of the Swiss and upper German Reformation.

This would change dramatically with the accession to the throne of Mary I (reigned 1553–58) and the reintroduction of traditional religion to England. However, Mary's reign had the unintended effect of increasing the Reformed influence on English Protestantism. Many of those who went into exile during her reign settled in areas influenced theologically by Calvin and his followers: Geneva itself, but also Emden and Frankfurt-am-Main. Mary's successor, her half-sister Elizabeth I (reigned 1558–1603), was implacably opposed to Calvin's theology, not least on account of its call for the radical separation of church and state, but many of her theologians and churchmen were strongly drawn to his teachings. The most "godly" among them sought to implement his teachings irrespective of the queen's opposition. These Puritans, as they have often been called, would radically shape the English church, and indeed English history, in the course of the seventeenth century. Groups of Puritan exiles would take

Calvin's teachings across the Atlantic to the newly formed American colonies.

One of the best-known Marian exiles was John Knox, who was to become one of Scotland's most influential reformers. As an exile in Geneva, Knox published a liturgical handbook in English, the *Book of Geneva* (1556). On his return to Scotland, probably later that year, he contributed to the reform of the Scottish church on Calvinist principles. This took place under the leadership of a group of Scottish nobles, and against the wishes of Mary, Queen of Scots (reigned 1542–67). The Reformation was introduced into Scotland in 1559, but the queen and those of her courtiers who wished were allowed to continue to worship according to Catholic tradition. Knox's *Book of Discipline* (1560) laid down the principles and structures of a national church ordered according to Calvin's theology and ecclesiology. The *Book of Geneva*, renamed the *Book of Common Order*, became the worship book of the Scottish church in 1564. Knox envisaged a national church ordered under superintendents appointed by local parishes. However, these superintendents were seen as equivalent to bishops and thus as crown appointments by Scotland's regent and later by its king, James VI of Scotland (reigned in Scotland 1567–1625; also James I of England 1603–25). The struggle over church order would feed into the civil war which racked Scotland and England during the seventeenth century. It would ultimately leave Scotland with a form of church government in which regional presbyteries replaced the superintendents.

The formation of the Netherlands was in many ways a testimony to the victory of Calvinist and Reformed influence. The Spanish Netherlands (roughly consisting of today's Netherlands, Belgium and Luxembourg) was made up of seventeen provinces, including more than 200 cities. It was the most thriving commercial area of Europe. The area found itself subject to the spreading influence of the Habsburgs: the southern French-speaking, or Walloon, provinces became Habsburg possessions by inheritance in 1477, while the northern, Germanic or Dutch, provinces were Habsburg by 1543. The Spanish Netherlands, and in particular the northern provinces, were an important centre of the *devotio moderna*. They had a well-organized educational system and there were active printing presses in many towns, which were not slow to publish works by Luther, Zwingli, Calvin and other reformers. Both Lutheran and more radical influences can be traced during the 1520s, and even after reforming interests were driven underground the Reformation continued to spread through conventicles, which were secret assemblies where the Bible was read and the new ideas discussed. By the 1530s, the Anabaptist movement was becoming more significant, under the influence of Melchior Hoffmann. Anabaptist Eucharists were being celebrated in Amsterdam by 1531, and the teaching of these groups was taken up by Bernhard Rothmann and Jan Matthijs, who moved to Münster when it was proclaimed the New Jerusalem in 1534. Many people from the northern Netherlands joined them. The siege and fall of Münster the following year led to the repression of Anabaptists in the Netherlands and to internal division within the movement.

Calvin's influence can first be identified in the 1540s, as churches began to be established in the southern provinces. These were influenced by ideas carried up the Rhine from Strasbourg, or brought from Zürich and Geneva, and also by the Huguenot refugees who fled France. Despite the efforts of Charles V to suppress them, the Reformed churches took hold in Antwerp. By 1554–55 both French- and Dutch-speaking congregations existed. The northern provinces first began to see organized Reformed congregations in the 1560s, often supported by pastors and literature sent from Emden. Through the 1560s, under Charles V's successor Philip II of Spain, the Reformed religion gained in popularity, and began to demand recognition and an end to persecution, including abolition of the Inquisition and suspension of edicts against heresy. In 1566 the regent, Margaret of Parma, passed an edict allowing Protestant worship to continue wherever it was already taking place, and later that year, despite a wave of iconoclasm, Calvinists and Lutherans were accorded the right to build churches in Antwerp, Amsterdam and Utrecht. However, just months later these rights were retracted by the regent, and Protestant churches were closed or demolished. Resistance to Spanish rule followed, particularly in the northern Netherlands. The early 1570s saw the seven northern provinces engaged in a struggle for political recognition. In 1581, they declared their independence as the Dutch Republic. Calvinism was deemed to be the "public church" although it was the church of a minority, and Catholicism was also tolerated. Calvinism was strengthened by a wave of Protestant refugees from the southern provinces after they were forcibly returned to Catholicism by Alexander Farnese in 1583. For the new Dutch state, the Reformed church represented an important aspect of its political existence.

Calvinism in the Low Countries tended to assert the faith as summarized in the Belgic Confession, accepted by a Synod in Antwerp in 1566. However, some theologians took a more positive attitude towards the abilities of the human free will than Calvin or the Belgic Confession. Jacob Arminius,

Professor of Theology at the University of Leiden, affirmed the position held by Erasmus that the human will could at least assent to salvation. After Arminius's death in 1609, his ideas were systematized and presented in the *Five Articles of the Remonstrants*. These were rejected by many followers of Calvin, and a controversy ensued which resulted in the calling of the Synod of Dordrecht, or Dordt, in 1618. The Synod rejected Arminius's position, affirmed the doctrine of predestination, and agreed what came to be seen as the five points of Calvinism: the total depravity of fallen human nature; the idea that the election of those chosen by God is unconditional on any action; the doctrine of limited atonement, that is, the teaching that the effect of Christ's atoning work was limited to the elect, and that God did not intend it for all; the conviction that God's grace is irresistible, so that no one could refuse it; and the belief that the saints, once elect, would persevere, and could not fall away. Although Arminianism persisted, particularly in England, where, in the eighteenth century, controversies between Calvinists and Arminians would mark the early years of Methodism, the Synod of Dordt, with its very specific interpretation of Calvin's doctrine of predestination, came to define mainstream Calvinism.

CONCLUSION

In the course of their lifetimes Martin Luther, John Calvin, and their reforming contemporaries initiated a religious revolution. It was a revolution which had profound implications on what people believed and how they expressed their faith. But it was a revolution which had implications also for the political organization of many parts of Western Europe.

At the beginning of the sixteenth century, and despite its regional differences, it is reasonable to speak of one Western church. By the end of the century, the church had fragmented and confessional differences had emerged. In them, the theology expounded by Luther and Calvin found practical and material expression. The style and furnishings of a church building, the language of the liturgy and of readings from Scripture, the clothes and the lifestyle of the priest, the music that was used (if any) and the hymns that were sung, the form of service, the presence of pictures and images, whether the people were offered communion in the form of bread alone or in the form of bread and wine: all these functioned as markers of a new distinction between Catholic and Protestant and of distinctions between different types of Protestantism. At the same time, these differences were not always clear-cut, and confessional distinctions were not always easy to perceive. For instance, the Church of England developed a particular form of Reformed doctrine, alongside ecclesiastical structures which still looked Catholic and a church–state relationship which seemed more Lutheran, or even Zwinglian; the church in southern German Württemberg developed a form of Lutheranism which in its church buildings and services looked remarkably Reformed; Lutherans in the city of Essen joined the Corpus Christi procession organized by the Catholics who lived outside their city, not because they believed in transubstantiation, but because they enjoyed a good celebration. Confessional differences could express themselves in idiosyncratic ways. Nonetheless, by the end of the sixteenth century, people recognized that these differences existed, and the ecclesiastical landscape had become consciously multifaceted.

Both Luther and Calvin developed their theology and their understanding of its practical implications in response to the specific circumstances in which they found themselves. Luther's theology emerged in a complex process, formed both by his own experience and by interaction with others, whether theologians, believers, or the local temporal authorities, with opponent or supporter (or even supporter turned opponent). He and his contemporaries laid the foundation for a new way of conceiving the church independent of papal hierarchy, much more focused on the importance of the individual's relationship to God. Calvin's theology was crafted in a world in which this alternative way of conceiving church was already taking shape. Calvin offered a more systematic way of conceiving that church experience and new insights into the implications of the evangelical theology.

The story does not end with Luther and Calvin. Many people played a part in helping the theological and practical concerns of these two men to spread and take shape across the continent and beyond. As they were taken into new contexts, Luther's and Calvin's ideas in turn changed and developed. The history of the religious changes which made up the Reformation is the story of a much more complex process of theological change than a focus on Luther and Calvin can begin to describe. Theologians, pastors, and lay people across Europe contributed to the shaping of the Reformation churches. Moreover, as should have become clear, this was not just a question of the influence of theologians. Territorial rulers and city councils were of central importance in initiating religious change. The changes in the beliefs and practice of religion were not only religious but profoundly political. The Reformation re-drew not only the ecclesiastical, but also the political map of Europe. It had important implications for defining what a state is and what it does. In most parts of Western Europe by the end of the sixteenth century, political identity and confessional identity were intricately entwined.

The era of the Reformation had a lasting impact in Europe. This religious revolution shaped the political and confessional landscape in ways which had far-reaching effects. The critique of the authority of the papacy and the appeal to the authority of Scripture challenged patterns of authority in ways which the Thirty Years War and processes of confessionalization proved the church to be unable to respond. The questions raised by Luther and Calvin and their fellow reformers laid foundations for the questions raised by enlightenment thinkers such as Descartes, Leibniz, and even Newton. Luther and Calvin were indeed religious revolutionaries, but the effects of their revolution reached far beyond religion or the church.

FURTHER READING

There are many works on Luther, Calvin and the Reformation, not all of which are in English. This book is much indebted to German language scholarship relating to Luther and Calvin, and to the spread of Lutheranism. However, only English language works will be mentioned here.

The standard (and comprehensive) biography of Martin Luther is the three-volume work by Martin Brecht, *Martin Luther* (Philadelphia: Fortress Press, 1985–93). More recent, and shorter, accounts are offered by Martin Marty, *Martin Luther* (New York: Viking Adult, 2004) and Michael A. Mullett, *Martin Luther* (London: Routledge, 2004). Robert Kolb, *Martin Luther: Confessor of the Faith* (Oxford: Oxford University Press, 2009) explores the development of Luther's theology in the context of his life. Still useful is Bernhard Lohse, *Martin Luther: An Introduction to His Life and Work* (Edinburgh: T&T Clark, 1987). Good summaries of important aspects of Luther's theology offered by a range of Luther scholars can be found in *The Cambridge Companion to Martin Luther*, edited by Donald K. McKim (Cambridge: Cambridge University Press, 2003). English translations of many of Luther's works are found in *Luther's Works* (St Louis: Concordia Publishing, 1974); fifty-five volumes are currently available, comprising about one-third of Luther's writings. A further twenty volumes are planned.

In 2009, a plethora of publications relating to the life and work of John Calvin appeared, to mark the 500th anniversary of his birth. For his biography, see Bernard Cottret, *Calvin: A Biography* (Grand Rapids: Eerdmans Publishing, 2000) or, more recently, Bruce Gordon, *Calvin* (New Haven: Yale University Press, 2009). A useful introduction is offered by Willem van 't Spijker, *Calvin: A Brief Guide to His Life and Thought* (Louisville: Westminster John Knox Press, 2009). Both *The Cambridge Companion to John Calvin*, edited by Donald K. McKim (Cambridge: Cambridge University Press, 2004), and *The Calvin Handbook*, edited by Herman J. Selderhuis (Grand Rapids: Eerdmans Publishing, 2009), offer summaries of key aspects of Calvin's theology by renowned scholars in the field. The development of Calvin's theology is traced in Richard A. Muller, *The Unaccommodated Calvin: Studies in the Formation of a Theological Tradition* (New York: Oxford University Press, 2000). English translations of a number of Calvin's works exist. This book has focused on three different versions of Calvin's *Institutes*: *Institutes of the Christian Religion: 1536 Edition*, translated and annotated by Ford Lewis Battles (Grand Rapids: Eerdmans Publishing, revised edition, 1986); *Institutes of the Christian Religion: 1541 French Edition*, translated by Elsie Anne McKee (Grand Rapids: Eerdmans Publishing, 2009); *Institutes of the Christian Religion* (1559 edition), translated by F. L. Battles and edited by J. T. McNeill (Louisville: Westminster John Knox Press, 1960; Library of Christian Classics, vols 20–21). The political aspects of Geneva's Reformation are presented in William G. Naphy, *Calvin and the Consolidation of the Genevan Reformation* (Manchester: Manchester University Press, 1994). For the spread of Calvinism and the Reformed tradition, see Graeme Murdock, *Beyond Calvin: The Intellectual, Political and Cultural World of Europe's Reformed Churches* (Basingstoke: Palgrave Macmillan, 2004).

The wider scope of the Reformation is addressed by Diarmaid MacCulloch, *Reformation: Europe's House Divided, 1490–1700* (London: Penguin, 2003). Patrick Collinson, *The Reformation* (London: Wiedenfeld & Nicolson, 2003) offers a briefer summary, including a helpful discussion of different ways that the Reformation has been interpreted by historians. Carter Lindberg's textbook, *The European Reformations* (Oxford: Blackwell, 1996) has a useful companion volume of primary sources: *The European Reformations Sourcebook* (Oxford: Wiley-Blackwell, 2000). Brief introductions to the lives and thought of a range of reformers are given in *The Cambridge Companion to Reformation Theology*, edited by David Bagchi and David C. Steinmetz (Cambridge: Cambridge University Press, 2004), and *The Reformation Theologians: An Introduction to Theology in the Early Modern Period*, edited by Carter Lindberg (Oxford: Blackwell, 2002). *The Reformation World*, edited by Andrew Pettegree (London: Routledge, 2001), offers essays exploring the implementation of the Reformation in different areas of Europe, as well as the cultural and intellectual context.

INDEX